双语教材

Experience China
from Zhejiang

感知中国：从浙江出发

王晓华　徐蓓佳　王晓慧　吴雅云 编著

浙江工商大学 出版社 | 杭州
ZHEJIANG GONGSHANG UNIVERSITY PRESS

图书在版编目（CIP）数据

感知中国：从浙江出发：汉、英 ／ 王晓华等编著
. — 杭州：浙江工商大学出版社，2024.9
ISBN 978-7-5178-6043-3

Ⅰ．①感… Ⅱ．①王… Ⅲ．①汉语－对外汉语教学－
高等学校－教材 Ⅳ．① H195.4

中国国家版本馆 CIP 数据核字（2024）第 102875 号

感知中国：从浙江出发
GANZHI ZHONGGUO：CONG ZHEJIANG CHUFA
王晓华　徐蓓佳　王晓慧　吴雅云 编著

策划编辑	任晓燕
责任编辑	熊静文　王　英
责任校对	李远东　林莉燕
封面设计	浙信文化
责任印制	祝希茜
出版发行	浙江工商大学出版社
	（杭州市教工路 198 号　邮政编码 310012）
	（E-mail：zjgsupress@163.com）
	（网址：http://www.zjgsupress.com）
	电话：0571-88904980，88831806（传真）
排　　版	杭州彩地电脑图文有限公司
印　　刷	杭州高腾印务有限公司
开　　本	710 mm×1000 mm　1/16
印　　张	15
字　　数	164 千
版 印 次	2024 年 9 月第 1 版　2024 年 9 月第 1 次印刷
书　　号	ISBN 978-7-5178-6043-3
定　　价	68.00 元

前　言

　　习近平总书记在党的二十大报告中强调，要加快建设"教育强国、科技强国、人才强国"。这是党和国家首次将教育、科技和人才放在战略任务中进行统筹部署，并将教育放在首要位置。教育高质量发展在新的历史时期的重要性可见一斑。教育对外开放是中国教育高质量发展的重要方面。新时代新征程，作为我国教育对外开放的有机组成部分，来华留学教育事业需更加主动地融入国家发展大局，为提升中国教育的核心竞争力和国际影响力、深化国际科技与人文交流做出应有贡献。本书是浙江省内第一部以留学生为主要教学和阅读对象的中国概况类教材，也可供中外学生混合式课堂使用。作为世界著名的东方古国，中国每年吸引了大量的留学生，中国已成为亚洲最大的留学目的国。来华留学生是中国大学生群体的重要组成部分，也是中国高等教育事业国际化的重要实践者。留学生来到中国，既会对这个神秘的东方古国充满好奇，也会因面对一个陌生的环境而感到紧张。帮助留学生了解中国文化，体验中国社会，一方面有助于学生尽快适应在华学习生活，另一方面也是中国文化"走出去"的重要途径。因此，为留学生开设中国文化、

经济和社会生活方面的课程是非常必要且迫切的。

近年来，我国招收留学生的院校基本都开设了"中国概况"等文化课程。但是，目前的课程设计一般都侧重对中国历史文化的介绍，系统介绍当代中国全景全貌的课程较少，相关教材更是欠缺。这也是我们编写这部教材的初衷。本教材的特点主要有：

第一，内容全面。本教材不是关于中国某一个阶段，或者某一个方面的介绍，而是将历时和共时统一起来，旨在给留学生提供较为系统全面的社会文化知识。因此，本教材既包括历史文化类的主题（如朝代变迁、历史瞬间、儒家道家、少数民族等），也包括社会生活类的主题（如节日与节礼、文化休闲、五彩中国、百姓日常等），更有大量关于社会发展的主题（如教育科技、对外贸易、电子商务、百年企业）。

第二，强调感知。"纸上得来终觉浅，绝知此事要躬行"，我们的教学团队重视学生在文化课程中的体验和感知，希望通过"课上学、课后行、课外看"的教学方式，让学生真正做到感知中国。因此，本教材在编排上设计了四个感知板块，分别是：感知中国历史、感知中国习俗、感知中国社会和感知中国经济。

第三，立足浙江。浙江是中国古代文明的发祥地之一，拥有悠久的历史和深厚的文化底蕴。同时，浙江有较好的经济基础，拥有发达的制造业和现代服务业，更有一些在全国乃至全球都有影响力的企业。从浙江出发，以浙江为例，留学生可以全方位、多角度地感知中国。

此外，在教学与互联网深度融合的今天，本教材也希望在新形态方面有所探索。本教材的每一小节都有与教学内容相呼应的线上课程，师生可通过二维码获取。为了方便老师们及时有效地了解学生的学习情况，本教材不仅配有课堂思考与讨论，还为每小节设计了练习题，学生可通过在线问卷链接完成。

本教材由多位从事国际教育多年的一线教师合作编著而成，王晓华老师负责策划、总纂、体例设计以及统稿审稿，徐蓓佳老师带领张元勋、谌曾灵、许飞燕、高布克、叶卫挺等几位年轻教师完成了话题一第二章第二课及第三章第二课、话题二第一章第一课和第二课、话题三第二章第一课和第二课、话题四第一章第二课及第二章第一课和第二课，王晓慧老师完成了话题一第一章第一课及第二章第一课、话题二第二章第一课及第三章第二课、话题三第一章第一课、话题四第一章第一课及第三章第二课，吴雅云老师完成了话题一第一章第二课及第三章第一课、话题二第二章第二课及第三章第一课、话题三第一章第二课及第三章第一课和第二课、话题四第三章第一课。另外，胡根明先生慷慨提供了封面照片。

由于编者水平所限，本教材一定会有许多不足之处。因此，我们也盼望同行们提出宝贵的意见和建议，使本书在教学实践中得以优化。

编者

2024 年 2 月 20 日

目 录

CONTENTS

话题一 感知中国历史

第一章 朝代变迁 ·· 2

第一课 中国历史概述 ·· 2

第二课 古都临安 ·· 11

第二章 历史瞬间 ·· 19

第一课 主要历史事件和人物 ······························ 19

第二课 良渚遗址 ·· 29

第三章 儒家道家 ·· 40

第一课 中国人的宗教 ·· 40

第二课 南朝寺庙 ·· 49

话题二 感知中国习俗

第一章 节日与节礼 ·· 58

第一课 传统节日 ·· 58

第二课　浙江非遗 ……………………………………… 69

第二章　少数民族 …………………………………… **80**

第一课　少数民族简述 ………………………………… 80

第二课　畲族三月三 …………………………………… 89

第三章　文化休闲 …………………………………… **98**

第一课　汉字与书法 …………………………………… 98

第二课　绍兴酒与《兰亭序》 ……………………… 106

话题三　感知中国社会

第一章　五彩中国 …………………………………… **116**

第一课　中国的世界遗产 ……………………………… 116

第二课　浙江风采 ……………………………………… 126

第二章　百姓日常 …………………………………… **135**

第一课　中华美食 ……………………………………… 135

第二课　高铁去湖州 …………………………………… 143

第三章　教育科技 …………………………………… **153**

第一课　中国教育 ……………………………………… 153

第二课　国际生的网络生活 …………………………… 162

话题四　**感知中国经济**

第一章　对外贸易 ·················· **174**

　第一课　共建"一带一路" ·············· 174

　第二课　快递之乡 ·················· 182

第二章　电子商务 ·················· **191**

　第一课　跨境电商 ·················· 191

　第二课　阿里巴巴 ·················· 201

第三章　百年企业 ·················· **211**

　第一课　儒商浙商 ·················· 211

　第二课　胡庆余堂 ·················· 221

话题一　感知中国历史

● 第一章　朝代变迁

● 第二章　历史瞬间

● 第三章　儒家道家

第一章 朝代变迁

（中国长城 王晓华供图）

第一课 中国历史概述

更多讲解，请扫码观看

中国历史上下五千年，可划分为三个时期：古代史经历了原始社会、奴隶社会、封建社会三个阶段；近代史是从1840年第一次鸦片战争到1949年中华人民共和国成立；1949年至今为现代史。距今约170万年前的"元谋人"是目前中国境内已知最早的原始人类。始于公元前约 2070 年的夏朝为史书记载的最早王朝，商朝时期青铜文明繁荣，西周建立周礼，春秋战国时期诸侯称霸，思想学术活跃，涌现出老子、孔子、孟子、庄子、墨子等人物。秦朝建立于公元前 221 年，这是中国历史上第一个统一的多民族中央集权封建王朝。公元前 206 年汉朝建立，汉武帝在位期间开辟了"丝绸之路"，促进东西方交往和佛教的传入。此后经历了三国、晋、南北朝、隋等朝代。公元 618 年建立了唐朝，国力强盛，疆域辽阔，对外经济文化交流进一步发展。唐朝后经历了五代十国时期。公元 960 年宋朝建立，先后有北宋、南宋，文化、科技、经济高度繁荣。1206 年元建国，1271 年改国号为元。"四大发明"相继传入世界各地。1368 年明朝建立，迁都北京，郑和七下西洋，促进了海外贸易和文明交流。1616 年清建国，1636 年改国号为清，1644 年入关，开拓疆土，平定叛乱，安定西藏，收复台湾，奠定当代中国版图。1911 年孙中山领导辛亥革命结束了封建君主制，1912 年中华民国建立。1921 年，中国共产党诞生。1949 年 10 月 1 日，中华人民共和国正式成立。新中国成立初期土地改革和第一个五年计划成功完成，开始大规模建设社会主义。1978 年，中国决定推行改革开放政策，通过改革经济体制、政治体制，逐步确立具有中国特色的社会主义现代化建设道路。2022 年党的二十大谋划全面建设社会主义现代化国家，推进中国式现代化，并致力于推动构建人类命运共同体。中国呈现出政局稳定、经济高速发展、外交活跃的繁荣局面。

课堂思考与讨论

1. 把中国历史上的重要朝代与时间进行匹配连线。

秦朝　　　　　　　公元前 206 年

汉朝　　　　　　　公元 618 年

唐朝　　　　　　　公元前 221 年

宋朝　　　　　　　公元 1206 年

元朝　　　　　　　公元 1616 年

明朝　　　　　　　公元 1368 年

清朝　　　　　　　公元 960 年

2. 中国历史上有哪些繁荣的时期？如果有时光穿梭机，你最想去中国的哪个朝代看看，为什么？

3. 你对古代历史还是近、现代历史感兴趣？做课内或课外小调查，了解其他人对历史的兴趣。

4. 你对哪个中国历史人物感兴趣？查资料，进行人物介绍。

5. 你们国家有哪些著名的历史人物？选择其中一位进行介绍，或者将他/她与中国历史人物进行比较。

Overview of Chinese History

The history of China is around 5,000 years, which can be divided into three periods. The ancient history has gone through three stages: primitive society, slave society and feudal society. The history of modern China is from the First Opium War in 1840 to the founding of the People's Republic of China (PRC) in 1949. Since 1949, it has been the contemporary era. The "Yuanmou Man" who lived about 1.7 million years ago is the earliest known hominid in China. The Xia Dynasty, which began in about 2070 BC, is the earliest dynasty recorded in historical books. Bronze civilization flourished in the Shang Dynasty. The Western Zhou Dynasty established the rites of Zhou. The feudal lords in the Spring and Autumn Period and the Warring States Period dominated. The thoughts and academic activities were active, and Laozi, Confucius, Mencius, Zhuangzi, Mozi and other figures emerged. The Qin Dynasty was founded in 221 BC, which is the first unified multi-ethnic centralization feudal dynasty in history of China. In 206 BC, the Han Dynasty was established. During the reign of Emperor Wu of Han, the "Silk Road" was opened to promote east-west exchanges and the introduction of Buddhism. After that, came the Three Kingdoms Period, Jin Dynasty, Northern and Southern Dynasties, Sui Dynasty and other dynasties. The Tang Dynasty was established in 618 AD, with strong national power, vast territory and further development of external economic and cultural exchanges. After the Tang Dynasty, it went through the Five Dynasties and Ten Kingdoms Period. The Song Dynasty was established in

960 AD, including the Northern and Southern Song Dynasties, with a high degree of cultural, technological, and economic prosperity. In 1206, Yuan was founded, and in 1271, the whole country's name was changed to Yuan. "The Four Great Inventions" were introduced to different parts of the world successively. The Ming Dynasty was established in 1368, with the relocation of its capital to Beijing. Zheng He's seven voyages to the West promoted overseas trade and cultural exchange. Qing was founded in 1616, and changed the whole country's name to Qing in 1636, and entered Shanhaiguan Pass in 1644. It expanded its territory, quelled rebellions, stabilized Xizang, recovered Taiwan, and laid the foundation for the territory of contemporary China. In 1911, Sun Yat-sen led the Revolution of 1911 to end the feudal monarchy. In 1912, the Republic of China was established. In 1921, the Communist Party of China (CPC) was founded. On October 1, 1949, the People's Republic of China (PRC) was officially established. At the beginning of the founding of the People's Republic of China, the land reform and the first five-year plan were successfully completed, and large-scale socialist construction was carried out. In 1978, China decided to implement the reform and opening-up policy, gradually establishing a path of socialist modernization with Chinese characteristics through the reform of the economic and political systems. The 20th CPC National Congress in 2022 planned to build a modern socialist country in all aspects, promote Chinese modernization, and strive to promote the building of a community with a shared future for mankind. China has shown a prosperous situation of political stability, rapid economic development, and active diplomacy.

Think and discuss

1. Match the important dynasties in the history of China with the time.

Qin Dynasty   206 BC

Han Dynasty   618 AD

Tang Dynasty   221 BC

Song Dynasty   1206 AD

Yuan Dynasty   1616 AD

Ming Dynasty   1368 AD

Qing Dynasty   960 AD

2. What are the prosperous periods in the history of China? If there is a time shuttle, which dynasty in China would you most like to visit and why?

3. Are you interested in ancient history, modern or contemporary history? Conduct small surveys in or out of class to find out other people's interest in history.

4. Which Chinese historical figure are you interested in? Search for information and make introductions.

5. Who are the famous historical figures in your country? Select one of them to introduce or compare him/her with Chinese historical figures.

一、判断题

1. 老子、孔子、孟子等重要人物出现于中国春秋战国时期。（　　）

2. 汉朝时中国建立了历史上第一个统一的国家。（　　）

3. 中国历史可以分为古代史、近代史、现代史三个时期。（　　）

4. 史书上记载的中国最早的王朝是夏朝。（　　）

5. 中国特色社会主义现代化建设道路是从 1966 年开始确立的。

（　　）

二、单选题

1. 中国境内已知最早的人类生活在距今约_____以前。

A. 170 万年　　　　B. 100 万年　　　C. 50 万年

2. 当代中国版图是在_____奠定的。

A. 明朝　　　　　　B. 宋朝　　　　　C. 清朝

3. 在_____，中国开辟了"丝绸之路"。

A. 汉朝　　　　　　B. 唐朝　　　　　C. 秦朝

4. 中华人民共和国成立于＿＿＿年。

A.1921   B.1949   C.1911

5. ＿＿＿年，中国决定开始实行改革开放政策。

A.1978   B.1949   C.1990

After-class exercises

I. True or false

1. Laozi, Confucius, Mencius and other important figures appeared in the Spring and Autumn Period of China.   (　　)

2. During the Han Dynasty, the first unified country was established in Chinese history.   (　　)

3. Chinese history can be divided into three periods: ancient history, modern history and contemporary history.   (　　)

4. The earliest dynasty in China recorded in the history books is the Xia Dynasty.   (　　)

5. The decision to build a path of socialist modernization with Chinese characteristics was made in 1966.   (　　)

II. Single choice

1. The earliest known human beings in China were about _____ ago.

A. 1.7 million years   B. 1 million years   C. 500,000 years

2. The map of contemporary China was established in the _____.

A. Ming Dynasty   B. Song Dynasty   C. Qing Dynasty

3. In the _____, China opened the Silk Road.

A. Han Dynasty   B. Tang Dynasty   C. Qin Dynasty

4. The People's Republic of China was founded in _____.

A. 1921   B. 1949   C. 1911

5. In _____, China decided to carry out the policy of reform and opening-up.

A. 1978   B. 1949   C. 1990

（浙江杭州西湖白堤　吴雅云供图）

第二课　古都临安

更多讲解，请扫码观看

杭州市是中国浙江省的省会，浙江省经济、文化、科教中心，长江三角洲中心城市之一，也是中国的特大城市之一。自秦朝设郡县制以来，杭州已有两千多年的历史，更是五代吴越国和南宋时期的都城所在，自然风景秀丽，人文古迹众多。历史上，杭州曾先后被称作钱塘、临安等。

南宋临安府（今浙江杭州）是南宋时期的都城之一，也是南宋的政治、经济和文化

中心。历史上的临安府地处今杭州西南部，是一个自然环境优美、交通便捷的地方。临安府南倚凤凰山，西临西湖，北部、东部为平原，城市呈南北狭长的不规则长方形。南宋御街，是南宋都城临安府的一条主要街道。"上有天堂，下有苏杭"的美誉亦于当时形成。临安府的经济非常繁荣。当时，临安府的商业和手工业发达，特别是在丝绸、茶叶、陶瓷、金银器和药材等方面，临安府因此成为中国南方重要的经济中心之一。此外，临安府也是南宋时期的文化中心，这里有许多著名的文人，他们的诗歌、文章、书法和绘画等文化遗产亦影响深远。

21 世纪，杭州又一次崛起，成为中国的商业和经济中心，成为中国数字经济和互联网产业的重要城市，是中国最具活力和创新力的城市之一。

2016 年，杭州成功举办了二十国集团领导人第十一次峰会。2023 年，杭州成功举办了第 19 届亚运会。截至 2023 年，杭州市下辖 10 个市辖区、1 个县级市、2 个县，总面积 16850 平方千米，常住人口 1252.2 万人，实现地区生产总值 20059 亿元。

 课堂思考与讨论

1. 在地图上找到杭州，说一说它的地理位置。

2. 解释一下，为什么说"上有天堂，下有苏杭"。

3. 除了临安（今杭州），中国还有哪些古都？

4. 杭州有什么特产？

5. 你来过杭州吗？如果你来杭州旅游，你最想去哪儿看一看？为什么？

The Ancient Capital of Lin'an

Hangzhou is the capital of Zhejiang Province, the economic, cultural, scientific and educational center of Zhejiang Province, one of the central cities in the Yangtze River Delta, and one of the megacities in China. Since the establishment of the system of prefectures and counties in the Qin Dynasty, Hangzhou has a history of more than 2,000 years. It is also the capital of Wuyue of the Five Dynasties and the Southern Song Dynasty. It has beautiful natural scenery and numerous cultural relics. In ancient times, Hangzhou has been called Qiantang, Lin'an, etc.

Lin'an Prefecture of the Southern Song Dynasty (now Hangzhou, Zhejiang) was one of the capitals during the Southern Song Dynasty and also the political, economic, and cultural center of the Southern Song Dynasty. In history, Lin'an Prefecture was located in the southwest of present-day Hangzhou and was a place with beautiful natural environment and convenient transportation. Lin'an Prefecture was adjacent to the Fenghuang Mountain in the south, the West Lake in the west, and plains in the north and east. The city was in an irregular rectangular shape that is long and narrow from north to south. The Southern Song Imperial Street was a major street built in the capital city of Lin'an Prefecture during the Southern Song Dynasty. The reputation of "There is heaven above, Suzhou and Hangzhou below." was also formed at that time. The economy of Lin'an Prefecture was very prosperous. At that time, the commerce and handicrafts of Lin'an Prefecture were developed, especially in areas such as silk, tea, ceramics, gold and silver vessels, and medicinal herbs, making Lin'an Prefecture one of the important economic centers in the south. In addition, Lin'an Prefecture was also a cultural center during the Southern Song Dynasty, with many famous literati whose cultural heritage such as poetry, articles, calligraphy, and paintings still affects people today.

In the 21st century, Hangzhou has once again emerged as the commercial and economic center of China, becoming an important city for China's digital economy and internet industry, and one of the most dynamic and innovative cities in China.

In 2016, Hangzhou successfully held the 11th G20 Leaders' Summit, and the 19th Asian Games were held in Hangzhou in 2023. By 2023, Hangzhou has 10 municipal districts, 1 county-level city and 2 counties under its jurisdiction, with a total area of 16,850 square kilometers, a permanent resident population of 12.522 million, achiving a regional GDP of 2,005.9 billion yuan.

Think and discuss

1. Find Hangzhou on the map and introduce its geographical location.

2. Explain why it says "There is heaven above, Suzhou and Hangzhou below".

3. What are other ancient capitals in China besides Lin'an (now Hangzhou)?

4. What are the special local products of Hangzhou?

5. Have you ever been to Hangzhou? If you go to Hangzhou for a visit, which scenic spot would you most like to visit? Why?

课后练习

一、单选题

1. 杭州是_____的省会。

A. 浙江省　　　　B. 江苏省　　　C. 广东省

2. 杭州在中国历史上也叫_____。

A. 金陵　　　　　B. 北平　　　　C. 临安

3. 现在，_____成为中国的"互联网之城"，在数字经济和互联网产业方面表现出了强劲的活力和创造力。

A. 北京　　　　　B. 杭州　　　　C. 上海

4. 2023年，杭州成功举办了第19届_____。

A. 亚运会　　　　B. 奥运会　　　C. 大运会

5. 截至2023年，杭州市下辖_____个市辖区、1个县级市、2个县。

A. 9　　　　　　　B. 10　　　　　C. 11

二、填空题

1. 杭州是中国历史上_____和_____的都城所在。

2. _____是南宋都城临安的一条主要街道，也是现在杭州市有名的旅游景点。

3. 南宋临安府的经济非常繁荣，特别是在_____、_____、陶瓷、金银器和药材等方面。

4. 中国有句俗话，"上有天堂，_____"。

5. 2016 年，杭州成功举办了_____。

After-class exercises

I. Single choice

1. Hangzhou is the provincial capital of _____.

A. Zhejiang Province

B. Jiangsu Province

C. Guangdong Province

2. Hangzhou is also known as _____ in Chinese history.

A. Jinling   B. Beiping   C. Lin'an

3. Now, _____ has become China's "Internet City", demonstrating strong vitality and creativity in the digital economy and internet industry.

A. Beijing   B. Hangzhou   C. Shanghai

4. In 2023, Hangzhou successfully held the 19th _____.

A. Asian Games   B. Olympic Games   C. Universiade

5. By 2023, Hangzhou has _____ municipal districts, 1 county-level city, and 2 counties under its jurisdiction.

A. 9   B. 10   C. 11

II. Filling in the blanks

1. Hangzhou is the capital city of _____ and _____ in Chinese history.

2. _____ is a main street built in Lin'an, the capital of the Southern Song Dynasty, and is also a famous tourist attraction in Hangzhou today.

3. The economy of Lin'an Prefecture in the Southern Song Dynasty was very prosperous, especially in areas such as _____ , _____ , ceramics, gold and silver vessels, and medicinal herbs.

4. There is a Chinese saying, "There is heaven above, _____ ".

5. In 2016, Hangzhou successfully held _____ .

（浙江杭州西湖雷峰塔 吴雅云供图）

第二章 历史瞬间

（西安钟楼 王晓慧供图）

第一课 主要历史事件和人物

作为一个古老国度，中国在历史上历经多次朝代更替和民族交融，在不同时期发生了多次重大事件，也涌现出不少风云人物。

1. 秦统一六国。公元前221年，秦始皇嬴政结束了500多年来诸侯分裂战乱的局面，建立中国历史上第一个统一的多民族中央集权制国家，推行郡县制，统一文字、货币、度量衡等，奠定了中国政治制度的基本格局。

2. 丝绸之路。汉武帝派张骞出使西域，开辟了以长安（今西安）为起点，经甘肃、

更多讲解，请扫码观看

新疆，到中亚、西亚，并连接地中海各国的陆上通道，促进了商贸流通和文化交流。

3. 郑和下西洋。明代郑和远航西太平洋和印度洋，拜访了 30 多个国家和地区，这是中国古代规模最大、时间最久的海上航行，发展了海上丝绸之路。

4. 鸦片战争。两次鸦片战争发生于 19 世纪中期，这标志着中国近代史的开始。中国在战后丧失了部分领土和主权，成为半殖民地半封建社会。

5. 辛亥革命。孙中山领导的辛亥革命发生于中国农历辛亥年即公元 1911 年，推翻了清朝专制帝制，建立了共和政体，开创了完全意义上的近代民族民主革命，推动了中国社会变革。

6. 五四运动。该事件发生于 1919 年 5 月 4 日，以北京的青年学生为主，社会各阶层共同参与，通过示威游行、请愿、罢工等多种形式表达中国人民对帝国主义、封建主义的反对，引发各种新思潮进入中国。

7. 中国反法西斯战争。该战争即中国人民抗日战争，是指 20 世纪三四十年代中国抵抗日本侵略的一场民族性的正义战争。抗日战争始于 1931 年的九一八事变，共历时 14 年。中国抗战取得了胜利，捍卫了国家主权和领土完整。

8. 中华人民共和国成立。1949 年 10 月 1 日毛泽东主席宣布中华人民共和国成立，中国进入了社会主义革命和建设时期。中国共产党领导全国各族人民实现从新民主主义到社会主义的转变，恢复了国民经济并开展经济建设。

9. 改革开放。20 世纪 70 年代中国实施对内经济改革和对外开放的政策，之后该政策成为中国社会主义建设的一项根本方针，为社会主义事业发展提供了强大动力。改革开放也成为中国走向富强的必经之路。

 **课堂思考与讨论**

1. 把中国历史上的重要事件与重要人物进行匹配连线。

秦始皇　　　宣布中华人民共和国成立

毛泽东　　　领导辛亥革命

孙中山　　　建立中国历史上第一个统一的多民族中央集权制国家

郑和　　　　出使西域，为开辟丝绸之路做贡献

张骞　　　　多次进行海上航行，发展海上丝绸之路

2. 谈一谈你印象最深的中国历史事件，它有什么重要影响？

3. 中国历史上有哪些促进中外交流的重要事件，它们对现代社会有什么重要影响？

4. 课外采访，了解中国人对历史上重大事件的看法。

5. 你的国家历史上有什么重要事件？这些事件对你的国家产生了什么影响？试着选择其中之一进行介绍。

感知中国：从浙江出发

Important Events and Influential Figures in Chinese History

As an ancient country, China has experienced many dynasty changes and ethnic integration in its history. Many major events have occurred in different periods, and many influential figures have emerged.

1. Qin unified the six states. In 221 BC, Qinshihuang, formerly named Ying Zheng, ended over five hundred years of division and wars between the feudal lords, established the first unified multi-ethnic centralization country in the history of China, implemented the system of prefectures and counties, standardized characters, currency, weights and measures, and laid the basic structure of China's political system.

2. The Silk Road. Emperor Wu of Han sent Zhang Qian as an envoy to the Western Regions, opening a land channel starting from Chang'an (now Xi'an), passing through Gansu and Xinjiang, to Central Asia and West Asia, and connecting Mediterranean countries, which promoted commercial distribution and cultural exchanges.

3. Zheng He's voyages to the Western Ocean. During the Ming Dynasty, Zheng He sailed to the Western Pacific Ocean and the Indian Ocean, visiting over 30 countries and regions. It was the largest and longest sea voyage in ancient China and developed "The Maritime Silk Road".

4. The Opium Wars. The two Opium Wars, which took place in the mid-19th century, marking the beginning of China's modern history. China

22

lost part of its territory and sovereignty after the war and became a semi-colonial and semi-feudal society.

5. The Revolution of 1911. The Revolution of 1911, led by Sun Yat-sen, which took place in the year of 1911, the year of Xinhai in the Chinese lunar calendar, overthrew the autocratic monarchy of the Qing Dynasty, established a republican regime, created a modern national democratic revolution in full sense, and promoted the social change in China.

6. The May Fourth Movement. It occurred on May 4, 1919, which was mainly composed of young students from Beijing, with the participation of other social classes. Through various forms such as demonstrations, petitions, strikes, it expressed the Chinese people's opposition to imperialism and feudalism, triggering various new ideological trends to China.

7. China's Anti-Fascist War. It is also called the Chinese People's War of Resistance Against Japanese Aggression, referring to a national just war that China fought against Japanese aggression in 1930s and 1940s during World War II. Chinese People's War of Resistance Against Japanese Aggression began in the September 18 Incident in 1931 and lasted for 14 years. China won the war and defended its national sovereignty and territorial integrity.

8. The People's Republic of China (PRC) was founded. Chairman Mao Zedong announced that the PRC was founded on October 1, 1949, and China entered the period of socialist revolution and construction. The Communist Party of China (CPC) led the people of all ethnic groups in the country to realize the transformation from new democracy to socialism, restore the

national economy and carry out economic construction.

9. Reform and opening-up. This was a fundamental policy of China's socialist construction in the end of 1970s, including domestic economic reform and opening up to the outside world. It provided strong impetus for the development of the socialist cause and was a necessary path for China to become prosperous and strong.

 Think and discuss

1. Match important events with important historical figures.

Qinshihuang   announced the establishment of the People's Republic of China

Mao Zedong   led the Revolution of 1911

Sun Yat-sen   established the first unified multi-ethnic centralization country in Chinese history

Zheng He   visited the Western Regions and made contributions to the opening of the Silk Road

Zhang Qian   conducted multiple maritime voyages and developed the Maritime Silk Road

2. Talk about the events in the history of China that impressed you most.

What are its important influences?

3. What are the important events in the history of China that have promoted Sino-foreign exchanges and had an important impact on modern society?

4. Conduct extra-curricular interviews to find out the views of Chinese people on major events in history.

5. What important events have occurred in the history of your country? What impact do these events have on your country? Try to choose one of them to introduce.

课后练习

一、判断题

1. 秦始皇第一次统一了中国的文字。　　　　　　　　　(　　)

2. 丝绸之路是以新疆为起点的。 （   ）

3. 改革开放政策包括对内经济改革和对外开放。 （   ）

二、单选题

1. 中国历史上第一个统一的朝代建立于_____。

A. 公元前 221 年　　　　B. 公元 221 年　　　　C. 公元前 21 年

2. 在明代远航西太平洋和印度洋的是_____。

A. 张骞　　　　　　　　B. 郑和　　　　　　　　C. 秦始皇

3. 中国近代史开始的标志是_____。

A. 辛亥革命　　　　　　B. 抗日战争　　　　　　C. 鸦片战争

4. 中国在鸦片战争后失去部分领土和主权，沦为_____。

A. 殖民社会　　　　　　B. 封建社会　　　　　　C. 半殖民地半封建社会

5. 中国历史上的五四运动发生于_____年。

A. 1911　　　　　　　　B. 1919　　　　　　　　C. 1931

6. 抗日战争发生于 1931 年，前后历时_____。

A. 14 年　　　　　　　　B. 8 年　　　　　　　　C. 4 年

After-class exercises

I. True or false

1. Qinshihuang standardized the Chinese writing characters for the first time. (   )

2. The Silk Road began in Xinjiang. (   )

3. The reform and opening-up policy includes both domestic economic reform and opening-up to the outside world. (   )

II. Single choice

1. The first unified dynasty in Chinese history was founded in _____.

A. 221 BC   B. 221 AD   C. 21 BC

2. In the Ming Dynasty, _____ made multiple voyages to the Western Pacific Ocean and the Indian Ocean.

A. Zhang Qian   B. Zheng He   C. Qinshihuang

3. The beginning of modern Chinese history is marked by _____.

A. the Revolution of 1911

B. Chinese People's War of Resistance Against Japanese Aggression

C. the Opium War

4. China lost part of its territory and sovereignty after the Opium War and became a _____.

A. colonial society

B. feudal society

C. semi-colonial and semi-feudal society

5. The May fourth Movement in Chinese history took place in _____.

A. 1911   B. 1919   C. 1931

6. Chinese People's War of Resistance Against Japanese Aggression took place in 1931 and lasted for _____.

A. 14 years   B. 8 years   C. 4 years

（秦始皇陵兵马俑　王晓慧供图）

（良渚遗址　王晓华供图）

第二课　良渚遗址

　　良渚，古代汉语中的意思是美丽的小洲，坐落在杭州市北郊余杭区。在良渚发现的古代城市遗址展现了中华文明乃至东亚地区史前稻作文明发展的极高成就。5500年前的一次全球大降温，使气候由暖湿变为干凉，这次降温迫使人们向平原低地迁徙，生产生活方式发生转变，农业逐渐取代渔猎采集成为主要生产模式。良渚时期，农业生产工具呈现出了多样化、专业化与规范化的特征，出

更多讲解，请扫码观看

现了成套的先进生产工具，犁耕使用普遍；水稻生产规模大，粮食产量也较高，在莫角山宫殿区南面的池中寺遗址，炭化稻谷仓储量约达39万斤。良渚时期，手工业也有很高的成就，玉器制作、制陶、木作、竹器编织、丝麻纺织都达到较高水平。玉器的制作技艺达到了一个新的高度，在琮、璧、钺等玉器上表现得尤为突出。这些玉器的质量、数量、体积、种类以及雕刻工艺均展现了中国史前的卓越治玉技术。这种高超的技术不仅塑造了璀璨的玉文化，也催生了一套独特的玉礼制度。值得一提的是，在位于良渚古城的外围发现了规模庞大的水利系统，这是目前已知的中国第一座大型水利工程，同时也是世界上最早的水坝系统。这个水坝系统的历史可以追溯到约4700至5100年前。这一发现进一步证明了良渚古城拥有完备的城市布局，包括宫城、王城、外郭城以及外围的水利系统。这使得良渚古城的价值能够与同时代的其他世界文明媲美。

良渚古城遗址特色景点包括：

1. 南城墙。在遗址的四面城墙上发现了8座水城门，在南城墙上发现了唯一的陆地城门。良渚先民在这里人工堆筑了3个台地，将此处划分成了4条通道，通过这些通道就可以进出城。

2. 钟家港。钟家港的钢网雕塑给人印象最深刻，这些雕塑栩栩如生，展现了当时的生活与生产，代入感极鲜明，还原了良渚古城当时的生活场景。

3. 莫角山宫殿区。莫角山台地是良渚时期最高统治者的宫殿区，有大莫角山、小莫角山、乌龟山3座独立的宫殿台基和周围35座房屋。莫角山宫殿区是良渚国王居住的地方，在此地可以登高远眺。

4. 反山王陵。在反山王陵可以参观 11 座良渚大墓，11 座墓葬按南北两排分布，等级高的居中。其中出土的随葬品数量多、规格高、制作精，有玉、石、陶、象牙、嵌玉漆器等将近 4000 件。

5. 鹿苑。景区有很多小森林，草地也非常美，来鹿苑的小朋友非常多。可以带胡萝卜、苹果等去喂小鹿，与小鹿亲密互动。

 课堂思考与讨论

1. 找出与良渚文化同时期的坐落于其他国家的文化遗址，比较其成就。

2. 拍摄良渚遗址照片，为它设计一句广告语。

3. 古代文化的传承和创新同样重要吗？至少给出 5 个理由。

4. 杭州还有什么世界之最？

5. 画一张世界粮食分布地图。

Liangzhu Site

Liangzhu, which means a beautiful island in ancient Chinese, is located in Yuhang District, the northern suburb of Hangzhou. The ancient urban ruins found in Liangzhu show the great achievements of the development of Chinese civilization and even the prehistoric rice-cultivating civilization in East Asia. 5,500 years ago, a global cooling occurred, with the climate changing from warm and humid to dry and cool. This cooling forced people to migrate to plains and lowlands, resulting in a shift in production and lifestyle. Agriculture gradually replaced fishing, hunting, picking and gathering as the main production model. During the Liangzhu Period, agricultural production tools showed characteristics of diversification, specialization and standardization, with the emergence of a complete set of advanced production tools. Plow farming had been widely used. The scale of rice production was large, and the grain yield was also high. In the Chizhongsi Site, south of the Mojiaoshan Palace District, the storage capacity of carbonized rice reached about 390,000 jin (a unit of weight, equal to half kilogram). During the Liangzhu Period, the handicraft industry had also made great achievements. Jade production, pottery making, carpentry, bamboo weaving, silk and linen weaving had all reached a high level. Especially for jade artifacts represented by cong, bi, and yue, their quality, quantity, volume, variety, and carving techniques had reached a peak in the level of prehistoric jade making in China, forming a brilliant jade culture and jade ritual system. It is worth mentioning that water conservancy system discovered outside the ancient city of Liangzhu is the earliest known large-scale water conservancy project in China and the earliest dam system in the world, dating back 4,700 to 5,100 years.

The water conservancy system indeed confirmed that the ancient city of Liangzhu had a complete urban layout, with palace district, royal district, outer district, and peripheral water conservancy system from the inside out. Its value was comparable to other world civilizations of the same period.

The characteristic attractions of the Liangzhu Ancient City Site include:

1. South City Wall. Eight water gates have been discovered on the four walls of the site, while the only land gate has been discovered on the southern wall. The ancestors of Liangzhu artificially built three terraces here, dividing it into four channels through which one could enter and exit the city.

2. Zhongjiagang. The steel mesh sculptures in Zhongjiagang are the most impressive. These sculptures are lifelike, vividly showcasing life and production of the time, with a strong sense of immersion, and restoring the living scenes of the ancient city of Liangzhu at that time.

3. Mojiaoshan Palace District. The Mojiaoshan Terrace was the palace area of the highest ruler during the Liangzhu Period, with three independent palace bases of Damojiao Mountain, Xiaomojiao Mountain, and Wugui Mountain, as well as 35 surrounding house ruins. The Mojiaoshan Palace District is the residence of King Liangzhu, where one can climb high and overlook.

4. Fanshan Royal Tomb. Fanshan Royal Tomb allows visitors to visit 11 Liangzhu tombs, which are arranged in two rows in the north and south, with the highest ranking in the center. Among them, there are a large

number of unearthed burial objects with high specifications and exquisite craftsmanship, including nearly 4,000 pieces of jade, stone, pottery, ivory, jade inlaid lacquerware and so on.

5. Luyuan. There are many small forests and beautiful grasslands in the scenic area, and many children come to Luyuan. Visitors can bring carrots, apples, etc. to feed the deer and interact closely with them.

 ## Think and discuss

1. Identify sites located in other countries during the same period of Liangzhu Culture and compare their achievements.

2. Take photos of the Liangzhu Site and design an advertising slogan for it.

3. Is the inheritance of ancient culture as important as innovation? Provide at least five reasons.

4. What else is the world's record in Hangzhou?

5. Draw a map of the world's food distribution.

课后练习

一、填空题

1. 良渚在古代汉语中的意思是＿＿＿＿＿。

2. 良渚时期，农业生产工具呈现出＿＿＿＿＿、＿＿＿＿＿、

＿＿＿＿＿的特征。

3. 良渚古城外围水利系统，是世界最早的水坝系统，距今已经有

＿＿＿＿＿年历史。

4. 良渚古城具有完整的城市布局，由内而外依次为＿＿＿＿＿、

＿＿＿＿＿、＿＿＿＿＿和＿＿＿＿＿。

5. 良渚古城遗址有特色景点＿＿＿＿＿，其中的钢网雕塑栩栩如

生，还原了良渚古城当时的生活场景。

二、单选题

良渚遗址坐落于＿＿＿＿。

A. 浙江省金华市

B. 江苏省南京市

C.浙江省杭州市

D.陕西省西安市

三、多选题

1.良渚玉器的品质、数量、体积、种类以及雕琢工艺达到了中国史前治玉水平的一个高峰，代表玉器有_____。

A.琮

B.璜

C.璧

D.钺

2.良渚古城遗址特色景点包括_____。

A.南城墙

B.莫角山宫殿

C.鹿苑

D.小瀛洲

3.以下哪种生活场景可以在当时的良渚古城见到？

A.种植水稻

B.种植小麦

C.使用石斧

D.制陶

4.莫角山台地是良渚时期最高统治者的宫殿区，有哪几座独立的宫殿台基？

A. 大莫角山

B. 中莫角山

C. 小莫角山

D. 乌龟山

After-class exercises

I. Filling in the blanks

1. Liangzhu means _____ in ancient Chinese.

2. During the Liangzhu Period, agricultural production tools showed the characteristics of _____ , _____ and _____ .

3. The outer water conservancy system of Liangzhu Ancient City is the earliest dam system in the world, with a history of _____ years.

4. Liangzhu Ancient City has a complete urban layout, from the inside out _____ , _____ , _____ and _____ .

5. The steel mesh sculptures in _____ are the most impressive, restoring the living scenes of the ancient city of Liangzhu at that time.

II. Single choice

Liangzhu Site is located in _____.

A. Jinhua City, Zhejiang Province

B. Nanjing City, Jiangsu Province

C. Hangzhou City, Zhejiang Province

D. Xi'an City, Shaanxi Province

III. Multiple choices

1. The quality, quantity, volume, type and carving techniques of Liangzhu jade have reached a peak level of jade making in prehistoric China, represented by _____ .

A. cong   B. pu

C. bi   D. yue

2. Liangzhu Ancient City Site's featured attractions include _____.

A. the South City Wall   B. the Mojiaoshan Palace

C. the Luyuan   D. the Minor Yingzhou

3. Which of the following life scenes can be seen in Liangzhu Ancient City at that time?

A. Growing rice.   B. Growing wheat.

C. Using stone axe.   D. Making pottery.

4. The Mojiaoshan Terrace was the palace area of the highest ruler during the Liangzhu Period. What are the three independent palace bases?

A. Damojiao Mountain.　　B. Zhongmojiao Mountain.

C. Xiaomojiao Mountain.　　D. Wugui Mountain.

第三章　儒家道家

（山东泰安岱庙　王晓华供图）

第一课　中国人的宗教

更多讲解，请扫码观看

中国人信仰的宗教主要有以下几种：

佛教。佛教是中国人信仰的主要宗教之一，在中国有着悠久的历史。佛教主张追求个人的灵性觉醒和超越世俗的束缚，并通过修行和禅定等方式实现。在中国，佛教的信徒很多，佛教有着广泛的影响力。

道教。道教是中国的本土宗教，它强调追求永生和超脱轮回，并认为可以通过修炼——修身、修心、修性、修行实现，其理论基础是道家思想。道家思想强调追求心灵的自由和内在的平静，主张追求超越现实和个体生命的永恒真理。道教吸收了古代神仙学、符咒术等元素，形成了自己独特的宗教体系和仪式。

基督教和天主教。这两种宗教在中国相对较新，但信仰者正在逐渐增多。此外，伊斯兰教在中国也有信众。

除了宗教之外，中国人的信仰还与中国哲学和中国文化相融合。

儒家思想。儒家学派创始人是孔子，儒家思想是中国文化中最具影响力的思想体系。儒家思想的主要特点是关注个人品德的培养和社会秩序的建立，强调人的自我完善和社会责任。儒家思想在中国历史上一直具有重要的影响力，尤其是在中国封建社会时期，统治者们将其作为治国理政的重要理论基础，并在教育领域广泛推广。

祖先崇拜。中国人的信仰中还融入了祖先崇拜文化。中国人的祖先崇拜文化可以追溯到古代，这是中国传统文化的重要组成部分。祖先崇拜是指人们对祖先的敬仰和礼仪，相信祖先在天之灵能够保佑后代平安幸福，也是一种尊重和感恩祖先的表现。中国的祖先崇拜文化与家庭有着密切的关系。在传统家庭中，祖先牌位是必不可少的，人们会在特定的日期进行祭拜，比如清明节、中元节、中秋节等，供上祭品，向祖先表达敬意和思念。中国人的祖先崇拜文化也是中国文化中一种特有的价值观和行为方式。

总的来说，中国的宗教信仰是多元的，不同的宗教有不同的信仰、教义和仪式，但它们都在不同的程度上对中国的文化、哲学和社会价值观产生了影响。

课堂思考与讨论

1. 你知道孔子吗？请介绍一下孔子。

2. 儒家思想对中国人的生活态度、生活方式以及社会道德准则产生了重大的影响。请用一个例子谈一谈你的理解。

3. 在你的国家，人民主要有哪些宗教信仰？

4. 介绍一个和宗教或者信仰有关的节日。

5. 佛教传入杭州始自东晋，盛于南宋。因此，杭州有很多有名的佛教寺庙。请说出至少一座杭州寺庙的名字。

Chinese Religion

The following are the main religions that Chinese people believe in :

Buddhism. Buddhism is one of the main religions believed by Chinese people, and it has a long history in China. Buddhism advocates the pursuit of personal spiritual awakening and transcending worldly constraints, achieved through practices and meditation. In China, there are many followers of Buddhism and Buddhism has a wide influence.

Taoism. Taoism is a local religion in China. It emphasizes the pursuit of immortality and transcendent reincarnation, and believes that it can be achieved through cultivation, that is, cultivation of the body, mind, nature, and spiritual practice. Its theoretical foundation is Taoism thought, which emphasizes the pursuit of spiritual freedom and inner peace, advocating the pursuit of eternal truth that transcends reality and individual life. Taoism absorbs elements such as ancient theology and incantation, forming its own unique religious system and rituals.

Christianity and Catholicism. These two religions are relatively new in China, but the number of believers is gradually increasing. In addition, Islam also has followers in China.

In addition to religion, the beliefs of Chinese people also combine with many elements of Chinese philosophy and culture.

Confucianism. Founded by Confucius, Confucianism is the most influential ideological system in Chinese culture. The main characteristic of Confucianism is its focus on the cultivation of personal morality and the establishment of social order, emphasizing human self-improvement and social responsibility. Confucianism has always had an important influence in the history of China. Especially in the feudal period, the rulers took it as an important theoretical basis for governing the country, and widely promoted it in the field of education.

Ancestor worship. Ancestor worship culture is also integrated into Chinese belief. Chinese ancestor worship culture can be traced back to ancient times, which is an important part of Chinese traditional culture. Ancestor worship refers to people's respect and etiquette for their ancestors, and people believes that their ancestors in heaven can protect the safety and happiness of future generations. It is also a manifestation of respect and gratitude for their ancestors. China's ancestor worship culture is closely related to the family. In traditional families, ancestral tablets are indispensable. People will worship on specific dates, such as the Tomb-Sweeping Festival, the Zhongyuan Festival, and the Mid-Autumn Festival, and offer sacrifices to honor their ancestors. The Chinese ancestor worship culture is also a unique value and behavior in Chinese culture.

Overall, the religion and beliefs of Chinese people are diverse. Different religions have different beliefs, teachings, and rituals, but they all have had an impact on China's culture, philosophy and social values to varying degrees.

 Think and discuss

1. Do you know Confucius? Please introduce Confucius.

2. Confucianism has had a significant impact on the living attitude, lifestyle, and social moral standards of Chinese people. Please provide an example to discribe your understanding.

3. Please introduce the main religion and beliefs of the people in your

country.

4. Introduce a festival related to a religion or belief.

5. Buddhism in Hangzhou began in the Eastern Jin Dynasty and flourished in the Southern Song Dynasty. Therefore, there are many famous Buddhist temples in Hangzhou. Please tell the name of at least one temple in Hangzhou.

单选题

1. _____是中国人信仰的主要宗教之一，它在中国有着悠久的历史。它主张追求个人的灵性觉醒和超越世俗的束缚，并通过修行和禅定等方式实现。

A. 佛教　　　　B. 道教　　　　C. 儒家思想

2. ＿＿＿是中国的本土宗教，它强调追求永生、长生和超脱轮回，并认为可以通过修炼道德、行功、修心和修身等方法实现。

A. 佛教　　　　B. 道教　　　　C. 儒家思想

3. ＿＿＿吸收了中国古代神仙学、符咒术等元素，形成了自己独特的宗教体系和仪式。

A. 佛教　　　　B. 道教　　　　C. 儒家思想

4. ＿＿＿的创始人是孔子，它是中国文化中最具影响力的思想体系。

A. 佛教　　　　B. 道教　　　　C. 儒家思想

5. 道教的理论基础是＿＿＿。

A. 道家思想　　　B. 儒家思想　　　C. 祖先崇拜

6. ＿＿＿是指人们对祖先的敬仰和礼仪，相信祖先在天之灵能够保佑后代平安幸福，也是一种尊重和感恩祖先的表现。它也是中国传统文化的重要组成部分。

A. 道家思想　　　B. 儒家思想　　　C. 祖先崇拜

7. 下面哪一个传统节日体现了中国的祖先崇拜文化？

A. 清明节　　　　B. 端午节　　　　C. 春节

8. ＿＿＿，民间俗称"七月半"，主要民俗活动有祭祖、放河灯等。它是追怀先人的一种传统节日。

A. 清明节　　　　B. 中秋节　　　　C. 中元节

After-class exercises

Single choice

1. _____ is one of the main religions believed by Chinese people, and it has a long history in China. It advocates the pursuit of personal spiritual awakening and transcending worldly constraints, and is achieved through practices and meditation.

A. Buddhism   B. Taoism   C. Confucianism

2. _____ is a local religion in China that emphasizes the pursuit of immortality and transcendent reincarnation, and believes that it can be achieved through cultivation, that is, cultivation of the body, mind, nature, and spiritual practice.

A. Buddhism   B. Taoism   C. Confucianism

3. _____ absorbs elements such as ancient Chinese ancient theology and incantation, forming its own unique religious system and rituals.

A. Buddhism   B. Taoism   C. Confucianism

4. The founder of _____ is Confucius, and it is the most influential ideological system in Chinese culture.

A. Buddhism   B. Taoism   C. Confucianism

5. The theoretical foundation of Taoism is _____.

A. Taoism thought   B. Confucianism   C. Ancestor worship

6. _____ refers to people's respect and etiquette toward their ancestors,

and people believes that the spirit of their ancestors in heaven can protect the safety and happiness of future generations. It is a manifestation of respect and gratitude toward their ancestors. It is also an important component of traditional Chinese culture.

A. Taoism   B. Confucianism   C. Ancestor worship

7. Which of the following traditional festivals reflects China's ancestor worship culture?

A. The Tomb-Sweeping Festival.

B. The Dragon Boat Festival.

C. The Spring Festival.

8. _____, commonly known as "July and a half" in folk customs, has main folk activities including offering sacrifices to the ancestors, sending river lanterns and so on. It is a cultural and traditional festival to commemorate the ancestors.

A. The Tomb-Sweeping Festival

B. The Mid-Autumn Festival

C. The Zhongyuan Festival

（山东曲阜孔庙　吴雅云供图）

（浙江杭州灵隐寺　徐蓓佳供图）

第二课　南朝寺庙

更多讲解，请扫码观看

"南朝四百八十寺，多少楼台烟雨中。"这是唐代诗人杜牧在《江南春》中写下的名句，描绘了江南地区佛寺林立的景象。比较有名的佛寺有南京栖霞寺、镇江金山寺等。那么，为什么南朝会有这么多的佛寺呢？这背后有着怎样的历史原因呢？

首先，我们要明确一下"南朝"的概念。南朝包括宋、齐、梁、陈4个王朝，它们均

以建康（今南京市）为都，上承东晋下启隋朝，共历 24 帝，计 169 年。南朝与北方的北魏、东魏、西魏、北齐、北周等北朝政权对峙，合称南北朝。

其次，我们要了解一下佛教在南朝的发展状况。在南朝时期，佛教得到了士族和民众的信仰和支持，尤其是在江南地区。皇帝和大臣都是虔诚的佛教徒，他们大兴土木，建造了许多寺院和塔院，供奉佛像和经典。《南朝寺考·序》记载："梁世合寺二千八百四十六，而都下乃有七百余寺。"可见当时佛寺之多。

杭州灵隐寺始建于东晋咸和元年（公元 326 年），占地面积约 87000 平方米。灵隐寺开山祖师为西印度僧人慧理和尚。南朝梁武帝赐田并扩建。五代吴越王钱镠命请永明延寿大师复兴开拓，并赐名灵隐新寺。

 **课堂思考与讨论**

1. 除了南京栖霞寺、镇江金山寺，南朝还有哪些著名的建筑？请举例。

2. 为什么南朝会有这么多佛寺？

3. 拍摄杭州灵隐寺的照片，并用一句话解说。

4. 中国寺庙建筑和其他国家的宗教建筑有什么区别？

Temples in the Southern Dynasties

"Four hundred and eighty splendid temples still remain; Of the Southern Dynasties in the mist and rain." This is a famous line written by the Tang Dynasty poet Du Mu in his poem *Spring in Jiangnan*, depicting the scene of numerous Buddhist temples in the Jiangnan region. Some well-known temples include the Qixia Temple in Nanjing and the Jinshan Temple in Zhenjiang. So, why are there so many Buddhist temples in the Southern Dynasties? What are the historical reasons behind this phenomenon?

Firstly, we need to understand the concept of the "Southern Dynasties". The Southern Dynasties include the Song, Qi, Liang and Chen dynasties, all of which had their capital in Jiankang (now Nanjing). They succeeded the Eastern Jin Dynasty and preceded the Sui Dynasty, with a total of twenty-four emperors and a span of one hundred and sixty-nine years. The Southern Dynasties were in opposition to the Northern Dynasties such as the Northern Wei, Eastern Wei, Western Wei, Northern Qi and Northern Zhou, collectively known as the Northern and Southern Dynasties.

Secondly, we need to understand the development of Buddhism in the Southern Dynasties. During this period, Buddhism gained support and devotion of the gentry and the common people, especially in the Jiangnan region. Emperors and officials were devout Buddhists, leading to a construction boom of temples and pagodas for the worship of Buddha statues and scriptures. According to the *Preface of the Record of Southern Dynasties' Temples*, there were "two thousand eight hundred and forty-six temples in the Liang Dynasty, and more than seven hundred temples in the capital region". This indicates the abundance of temples during that time.

The Lingyin Temple in Hangzhou was first built in the first year of the Xianhe era of the Eastern Jin Dynasty (326 AD), covering an area of approximately 87,000 square meters. The founding master of Lingyin Temple was the monk Huili from Western India, and it was expanded by the Emperor Wu of the Liang Dynasty. During the Five Dynasties, the king of Wuyue, Qian Liu, invited the master Yongming Yanshou to revitalize and expand the temple, giving it the name "Lingyin New Temple".

 Think and discuss

1. In addition to the Qixia Temple in Nanjing and the Jinshan Temple in Zhenjiang, what other famous buildings were there in the Southern Dynasties? Please give examples.

2. Why are there so many Buddhist temples in the Southern Dynasties?

3. Take a photo of the Lingyin Temple in Hangzhou and introduce it in

one sentence.

4. Discussion among Chinese and foreign students: What are the differences between Chinese temple architecture and other countries' religious architecture?

课后练习

一、填空题

1. 唐代诗人杜牧在《江南春》中写下的名句是"＿＿＿＿＿＿，多少楼台烟雨中"。

2. 比较出名的南朝寺庙有位于今镇江的＿＿＿＿＿＿和南京的＿＿＿＿＿＿。

3. 南朝包括＿＿＿＿＿＿、＿＿＿＿＿＿、＿＿＿＿＿＿、＿＿＿＿＿＿

4个王朝。

4. 灵隐寺位于浙江省_____市。

5. 灵隐寺的开山祖师为_____。

二、判断题

1. 南朝的4个王朝均以建康（今南京市）为都城。　　（　　）

2. 南朝时期，皇帝和大臣都是虔诚的佛教徒。　　（　　）

3. 南朝有很多出名的寺庙，其中包括烟雨楼。　　（　　）

4. 南朝梁武帝曾赐田扩建灵隐寺，并赐名灵隐新寺。　（　　）

5. 佛教是从印度传入中国的一种外来宗教。　·　（　　）

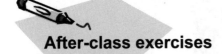

After-class exercises

I. Filling in the blanks

1. The Tang poet Du Mu once wrote a famous line "_____, of the Southern Dynasties in the mist and rain" in *Spring in Jiangnan*.

2. Notable temples of the Southern Dynasties include _____ in now Zhenjiang, and _____ in Nanjing.

3. The Southern Dynasties include the _____ , _____ ,
_____ , and _____ dynasties.

4. The Lingyin Temple is located in _____ , Zhejiang Province.

5. The founding master of Lingyin Temple is _____ .

II. Ture or false

1. All four Southern Dynasties had Jiankang (now Nanjing) as their
capital city. (　)

2. During the Southern Dynasties, both emperors and officials were
devout followers of Buddhism. (　)

3. The Southern Dynasties boasted many famous temples, including the
Yanyu Tower. (　)

4. Emperor Wu of the Liang Dynasty once granted land for the expansion
of the Lingyin Temple, renaming it the Lingyin New Temple. (　)

5. Buddhism is a foreign religion that originated in India and was
introduced to China. (　)

话题二　感知中国习俗

- 第一章　节日与节礼

- 第二章　少数民族

- 第三章　文化休闲

（中国春节　张元勋 供图）

第一章　节日与节礼

第一课　传统节日

更多讲解，请扫码观看

中国的传统节日不胜枚举，其中最有代表性的莫过于春节。春节即中国农历新年，俗称"新春"，又称"过年"，是集除旧布新、拜神祭祖、祈福辟邪、亲朋团圆、欢庆娱乐和饮食为一体的民俗大节。

春节时，人们都会穿上新衣服寓意辞旧迎新，颜色多为比较喜庆的红色，希望新的一年可以红红火火，寄托人们对新年的美好祝愿。民间春节吃饺子的习俗在明清时期已相当盛行。饺子一般要在大年三十晚上 12 点以前包好，待到半夜子时吃，这时正是农历正月初一的伊始。吃饺子取"更岁交子"之意，"子"为"子时"，"交"与"饺"谐音，有"喜庆团圆"和"吉祥如意"的意思。春节的习俗还有贴对联、放爆竹、吃年夜饭、守夜、拜年、收压岁钱等。对联是中国特有的民俗，也叫门对、春联、对子等，它采用大红纸张，以工整、对偶、简洁、精巧的文字描绘时代背景，抒发美好愿望。除夕夜放爆竹也有两千多年的历史，寓意吓走年兽，一年顺意。而年夜饭则象征着一年团圆，家庭和美。守岁由来已久，中国人在除夕有守岁的习惯，俗名"熬年"。新年前除夕夜晚守岁，民俗活动主要有点岁火、守岁火，即所有房子都遍燃灯烛，合家欢聚，迎接新年。拜年作为一种传统的中国民俗活动，已经成为人们在新年之初互相送上祝福的方式。拜年时，长辈会给晚辈派发压岁钱，寓意辟邪驱鬼，保佑平安。

关于春节的起源有几种说法，其中一种是腊（蜡）祭说。春节起源于上古时期的祭祀文化。腊是祭祀先祖，蜡是祭祀众神。古代劳动人民终年辛勤劳作，在年末收获时举行祭祀，感谢祖先和神明的庇佑，并祈求来年能够再获丰收。

春节虽定在农历正月初一，但春节的活动并不止于正月初一这天。春节活动一般从腊八节（农历十二月初八）开始，到元宵节（农历正月十五）结束。过腊八节意味着拉开了过年的序幕。在这一天，家家都要喝腊八粥。腊八粥主要由各种谷物和豆类熬制而成。农历十二月二十三或二十四，就是小年，祭灶是小年的传统习俗。灶指的是灶神、灶王爷。灶神受玉皇大帝之命监察人间并记录每户人家发生的事，并在腊月二十三这天回天宫汇报情况。为了讨好灶王爷，人们会贴灶王像并供奉饴糖等贡品，希望他在玉帝面前说好话，并祈求降福人间。之后人们便开始"忙年"——扫尘、购置年货、贴年红、洗头沐浴、张灯结彩等，

所有这些活动都有一个共同的主题，即"辞旧迎新"。

百节年为首、四季春为先，春节是中华民族最隆重的传统佳节。受中华文化的熏陶，世界上许多国家和地区都在庆祝春节。据不完全统计，已有近 20 个国家和地区的政府将中国春节定为法定节假日。其中，英国首都伦敦被视为对春节最为重视的西方城市之一。自 2006 年以来，伦敦已连续多年举行"中国在伦敦"的活动。近些年来，美国邮政、加拿大邮局每年发行中国农历新年邮票。

课堂思考与讨论

1. 哪些中国的传统节日和你国家的节日有相似之处？

2. 学完本课，你知道了哪些中国春节的传统习俗？

3. 除了春节的传统习俗外，你还了解哪些近年来在中国兴起的春节新习俗？

4. 随着社会的发展，一些传统的习俗逐渐被人们忘记，有哪些方法可以鼓励年轻人传承优秀传统文化？

5. 海外也有很多人庆祝中国春节，对于这个现象，你怎么看？

Traditional Festivals

There are countless traditional festivals in China, and the most representative one is the Spring Festival. The Spring Festival is the Chinese Lunar New Year, commonly known as "New Year", also known as "Guo Nian (spend the Spring Festival)". It is a folk festival that integrates the removal of old things and setting up new things, worship of gods and ancestors, praying for blessings and warding off evil spirits, family and friend reunions, celebration, entertainment and food.

During the Spring Festival, people will wear new clothes, symbolizing a farewell to the old and a welcome to the new. The colors are mostly festive red, hoping that the new year can be prosperous, expressing people's good wishes for the New Year. The custom of eating dumplings during the Chinese New Year was quite prevalent during the Ming and Qing dynasties. Dumplings are usually made before 12:00 p.m. on New Year's Eve and eaten in the middle of the night. This is the beginning of the first day of the first lunar month, and eating dumplings (jiaozi) means "Gengsui Jiaozi"(更岁交子). "Zi" means "zishi"(子时), and "交" is homophonic with "饺", meaning "happy reunion" and "good luck". The customs of the Spring Festival include pasting couplets, setting off firecrackers, eating New Year's Eve dinner, guarding the night, paying New Year's greetings, and collecting gift money. The couplet is a unique folk symbol in China, also known as the door couplet, spring couplet, antithetical couplet, etc. It uses bright red paper to depict the background of the times in neat, antithetic, concise and exquisite words, expressing good wishes. Setting off firecrackers on New Year's Eve has a history of over 2,000 years, symbolizing scaring away New Year's beasts and ensuring a smooth year. New Year's Eve dinner symbolizes reunion and family harmony throughout the year. Guarding the night has a long history, and the Chinese people have a habit of watching New Year's Eve, commonly known as "enduring the New Year". On New Year's Eve, the main folk activities are lighting a New Year's Eve fire and then watching it. That is, all houses are lit with lights and candles, and families gather to welcome the New Year. Paying New Year's greetings is a traditional Chinese custom, a way for people to express good wishes to each other at the beginning of the New Year. When paying New Year's greetings, elders will distribute gift money to younger generations, symbolizing the prevention of evil spirits and the protection of peace.

There are several stories about the origin of the Spring Festival. One of them is about the sacrifice. The Spring Festival originated from the sacrificial culture of ancient times. "La Sacrifice" is a sacrifice to ancestors, and "Zha Sacrifice" is a sacrifice to gods. The ancient working people worked hard all year round and held sacrifices at the end of the year to thank their ancestors and gods for their protection, and prayed for another bumper harvest in the coming year.

Although the Spring Festival is scheduled on the first day of the first lunar month, its celebrating activity is not limited to that day. Generally, it starts from the Laba Festival (the 8th day of the 12th lunar month) and ends with the Lantern Festival (the 15th day of the 1st lunar month). Celebrating the Laba Festival signifies the beginning of the Chinese New Year. On this day, every family has Laba Congee, which is mainly made from various grains and beans. The 23rd or 24th day of the 12th lunar month is Xiaonian. It is a traditional custom to offer sacrifices to the kitchen stove. The kitchen stove here represents the Kitchen God or the King of Kitchen. The Kitchen God is ordered by the Jade Emperor to oversee the human world and record what happens in each family, and report back to the Heaven Palace on the 23rd day of the 12th lunar month. In order to please the Kitchen God, people stick a picture of the Kitchen God and offer sacrifices such as candy, hoping that he can say good things about the family in front of the Jade Emperor and pray for blessings on the earth. Afterwards, people began to engage in "busy New Year" activities—sweeping dust, purchasing New Year's goods, pasting New Year's decorations, washing their hair and bathing, and decorating with lanterns and decorations, etc. All of these activities share a common theme, which is "bidding farewell to the old and welcoming the new".

With a hundred festivals, the Spring Festival is the most important, and among the four seasons, spring comes the first. The Spring Festival is the most solemn traditional festival of the Chinese nation. Influenced by Chinese culture, some countries and regions around the world also celebrate the Chinese New Year. According to incomplete statistics, nearly 20 countries and regions have designated the Chinese New Year as a legal holiday. London which is the capital of England is considered to be one of the western cities that pay the most attention to the Spring Festival. The "China in London" event has been held in London every year since 2006. In recent years, the American and Canadian Postal Service issue Chinese New Year stamps every year.

 Think and discuss

1. Which traditional Chinese festivals have similarities with those in your country?

2. After completing this lesson, what traditional customs do you know about the Spring Festival?

3. Besides the traditional customs of the Spring Festival, what other new customs that have emerged in China in recent years?

4. With the development of society, some traditional customs are gradually forgotten by people. What methods do you have to encourage young people to inherit excellent traditional culture?

5. Some people overseas also celebrate the Spring Festival. What do you think of this phenomenon?

课后练习

一、单选题

以下哪项不是春节的主要习俗？

A. 祭奠祖先

B. 除旧布新

C. 赛龙舟

D. 祈求丰年

二、多选题

1. 代表中国祥瑞文化的动物有哪几种？

A. 龙

B. 凤

C. 麒麟

D. 兔

2. 人们在端午节会做什么？

A. 赛龙舟

B. 吃粽子

C. 喝雄黄酒

D. 制陶

3. 中国其他民族的传统节日有哪些？

A. 壮族三月三

B. 中秋节

C. 傣族泼水节

D. 那达慕大会

三、判断题

1. 除夕是一年的第一天。（　　　）

2. 中秋节在每年的农历八月十五日。（　　　）

3. 重阳节的主题是祭祀祖先。（　　　）

4. 中国少数民族节日的文化内涵值得学习。（　　　）

After-class exercises

I. Single choice

Which is NOT the main custom of the Spring Festival?

A. Worship ancestors.

B. Eliminate the old and replace with the new.

C. Dragon Boat Race.

D. Pray for a good harvest.

II. Multiple choices

1. Which of the following animals represent Chinese auspicious culture?

A. Dragon.

B. Phoenix.

C. Kylin.

D. Rabbit.

2. What do people do during the Dragon Boat Festival?

A. Hold dragon boat races.

B. Eat zongzi.

C. Drink realgar wine.

D. Make pottery.

3. What are the traditional festivals of other ethnic groups in China?

A. The Sanyuesan Festival.

B. The Mid-Autumn Festival.

C. The Water-Splashing Festival.

D. The Nadam Fair.

III. True or false

1. New Year's Eve is the first day of the year. (   )

2. The Mid-Autumn Festival takes place annually on the 15th day of the 8th month in the Chinese lunar calendar. (   )

3. The theme of the Double Ninth Festival is to worship ancestors. (   )

4. The cultural connotations of Chinese ethnic minority festivals are worth learning. (   )

（龙泉青瓷　徐蓓佳供图）

第二课　浙江非遗

更多讲解，请扫码观看

　　中国非物质文化遗产，是指中国各族人民世代相传并视为其文化遗产组成部分的各种传统文化表现形式，以及与传统文化表现形式相关的实物和场所。包括：1.传统口头文学以及作为其载体的语言；2.传统美术、书法、音乐、舞蹈、戏剧、曲艺和杂技；3.传统技艺、医药和历法；4.传统礼仪、节庆等民俗；5.传统体育和游艺；6.其他非物质文化遗产。浙江省共有257项国家级非物质文化遗产代表性项目，最有名的包括：

龙泉青瓷烧制技艺。龙泉是浙江省历史文化名城，位于浙江西南部，与江西、福建两省接壤，以出产青瓷著称。龙泉青瓷制作过程包括8个关键步骤，分别是配料、成型、修坯、装饰、素烧、施釉、装匣、装窑以及烧制。特别值得一提的是，施釉和烧制这两个阶段具有独特之处。坯件经素烧干燥后施釉，施釉包括荡釉、浸釉、涂釉、喷釉等。厚釉类产品通常要施釉数层，施一层素烧一次，再施釉再素烧，如此反复四五次方可；最多者要施釉10层以上，然后才进入正烧。素烧温度比较低，一般在800摄氏度左右，而正烧则在1200摄氏度左右。青瓷烧制不仅是一种技术，而且是一种艺术。上乘青瓷青翠滋润、莹澈剔透，富于韵味，有"类玉"之美，体现出深厚的文化内涵。

水乡社戏。水乡社戏是浙江农村和城镇一种以戏剧表演为核心的民俗活动，它具有祭神和娱人相结合的特点，普遍流行于绍兴地区。就社戏而言，其演出程序相对稳定，主要遵循"闹场—彩头戏—突头戏—大戏—收场"的顺序。彩头戏和突头戏通常在白天上演，而大戏，也就是正戏，则从傍晚开始。大戏通常以历史剧和家庭剧为主，其间穿插的小戏有一定的规律。绍兴水乡社戏汇聚并展现了各种戏剧类型的表演风格，同时也充分展示了该地区丰富的民间文化。千百年来，绍兴水乡社戏除承担高台教化的任务外，还要发挥娱乐功能，由此逐渐发展成江南民间最隆重、最活跃、参与面最广的一种节日庆典活动。水乡社戏扎根民间，深受广大观众喜爱，至今仍可在绍兴地区的城市和乡村见到它的影踪。

剪纸（乐清细纹刻纸）。乐清市位于浙江东南沿海地区，乐清细纹刻纸是一门当地传承下来的技艺。乐清细纹刻纸的刀法精湛，线条刚劲有力，表现力十分丰富。其显著特征之一就是精致细腻。在早期的"龙船花"刻纸作品中，最微小的细节可以在一张一寸见方的纸上雕刻出52条线，制作一张大如碗口的精细刻纸需要花费10多天的时间。这种精细的刻纸技术使得各种民间图案和纹样能够在几厘米见方的纸上呈现出来。因此，乐清的细纹刻纸被称为"中国剪纸的南宗代表"。

 课堂思考与讨论

1. 非物质文化遗产的含义是什么？请进行解释。

2. 除了文章中提到的这些非遗项目外，你还知道哪些中国非物质文化遗产项目，请举例说明。

3. 学做一次中国剪纸，并和同学进行交流。

4. 你的国家有非物质文化遗产吗？请向大家介绍一个你的国家的非物质文化遗产项目。

Intangible Cultural Heritage in Zhejiang

Chinese intangible cultural heritage refers to various traditional cultural expressions that have been passed down from generation to generation by Chinese people of all ethnic groups and are considered as part of their cultural heritage, as well as physical objects and places related to traditional cultural expressions, including: 1. traditional oral literature and the language used as its carrier; 2. traditional art, calligraphy, music, dance, drama, folk art and acrobatics; 3. traditional techniques, medicine and calendars; 4. traditional etiquette, festivals and other folk customs; 5. traditional sports and entertainment; 6. other intangible cultural heritage. There are a total of 257 national intangible cultural heritage representative projects in Zhejiang Province. The most famous ones include:

Longquan Celadon Firing Technique. Longquan is a famous historical and cultural city in Zhejiang Province, located in the southwest of Zhejiang, bordering Jiangxi and Fujian provinces. It is famous for producing celadon. The production process of Longquan celadon includes nine steps, that is, preparing materials, forming, trimming, decorating, glazing, plain firing, boxing, kiln loading, and firing. Among them, the two steps of glazing and plain firing are very distinctive. After plain fire, the body is dried and then glazed. Glazing can be divided into several types, such as swinging glaze, soaking glaze, coating glaze, spraying glaze. Thick glazed products usually require several layers of glaze. After applying glaze, firing once; and then repeat the step. This process is repeated four or five times, with a maximum of ten or more layers of glaze before entering normal firing. The temperature for plain firing is relatively low, usually around 800 degrees Celsius, while for normal firing, it is around 1,200 degrees Celsius. Celadon firing is not only a technique, but also an art. High-quality celadon is green, moist, translucent and full of charm, with the beauty of jade, reflecting profound cultural connotations.

Shuixiang Social Drama. Shuixiang Social Drama is a folk activity centered on theatrical performance in rural and urban areas of Zhejiang Province. It combines the characteristics of worshipping gods and entertaining people, and is widely popular in Shaoxing. The performance routine of social drama is relatively fixed, and it is basically carried out in the order of "making a scene–caitou performance (mainly a lucky drama that congratulates one on wealth and promotion)–tutou performance (a drama that lays the foundation for the main play)–big performance–ending". Caitou and tutou performances are usually performed during the day, while big performance begins in the evening. Big performances are usually dominated by historical and family dramas, and some small dramas are interspersed in and relatively fixed. Shaoxing Shuixiang Social Drama combines and reflects the performance styles of different types of dramas, and fully showcases the rich and colorful local customs. For thousands of years, Shaoxing Shuixiang Social Drama has not only undertaken the task of education, but also played a role of entertainment, gradually developing into the most solemn, active and widely participated festival celebration activity among the people in Jiangnan. Shuixiang Social Drama is deeply rooted in the people and deeply loved by the general audience. Its traces can still be seen in cities and rural areas of Shaoxing to this day.

Paper Cuttings (Yueqing Fine Grain Paper Cutting). Yueqing City is located on the southeast coast of Zhejiang Province, and fine grain paper cutting in Yueqing is a local masterpiece. Yueqing fine grain paper cutting technique is exquisite, with strong and powerful lines and rich expressive power. One of its most prominent features is delicacy. In the early cutting of "Dragon Boat Flowers", the thinnest one could cut 52 lines on a piece of an-inch-square paper. A large bowl-shaped fine grain paper cutting take more than ten days, which is very labor-intensive. The technique of fine grain paper cutting makes all kinds of folk designs and patterns expressed in detail and on a piece of a-few-centimeter-square paper, which makes Yueqing fine grain paper cutting known as "the representative of the Southern School of Paper Cuttings in China".

 Think and discuss

1. Please explain what intangible cultural heritage means.

2. In addition to the intangible cultural heritage projects mentioned in the article, what other Chinese intangible cultural heritage projects do you know? Please give examples.

3. Learn to make Chinese paper cuttings and communicate with your

classmates.

4. Does your country have intangible cultural heritage? Please introduce a project of intangible cultural heritage in your country.

一、填空题

1.浙江省共有_____项国家级非物质文化遗产代表性项目。

2.浙江省著名的青瓷出自_____（地方）。

3.素烧温度比较低，一般在_____摄氏度左右，而正烧则在_____摄氏度左右。

4.水乡社戏主要遵循_____的演出顺序。

5.乐清细纹刻纸获得了"_____"之称。

二、单选题

我国的"文化遗产日"是哪一天?

A. 每年的 6 月 1 日

B. 每年 6 月的第 3 个星期五

C. 每年 6 月的第 2 个星期六

D. 每年的 6 月 13 日

三、多选题

1. 非物质文化遗产包括以下哪些方面?

A. 传统口头文学以及作为其载体的语言

B. 传统美术、书法、音乐、舞蹈、戏剧、曲艺和杂技

C. 传统技艺、医药和历法

D. 传统礼仪、节庆等民俗

E. 传统体育和游艺

2. 以下哪些是浙江省非物质文化遗产项目?

A. 龙泉青瓷烧制技艺

B. 水乡社戏

C. 乐清细纹刻纸

D. 绘画

3. 水乡社戏包括哪几场戏?

A. 闹场

B. 彩头戏

C. 目连戏

D. 突头戏

4. 以下哪些是中国非物质文化遗产项目？

A. 京剧

B. 太极拳

C. 针灸

D. 春节

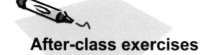

After-class exercises

I. Filling in the blanks

1. There are a total of _____ national representative intangible cultural heritage projects in Zhejiang Province.

2. The famous celadon in Zhejiang Province comes from _____ .

3. The plain firing temperature is relatively low, usually in _____ degrees Celsius, while normal firing is in _____ degrees Celsius.

4. Shuixiang Social Drama mainly follows the performance sequence of _____ .

5. Yueqing fine grain paper cutting has been known as _____ .

II. Single choice

Which date is China's Cultural Heritage Day ?

A. June 1st each year.

B. The 3rd Friday in June each year.

C. The 2nd Saturday in June each year.

D. June 13th each year.

III. Multiple choices

1. Which of the following aspects does intangible cultural heritage include?

A. Traditional oral literature and the language used as its carrier.

B. Traditional art, calligraphy, music, dance, drama, folk art, and acrobatics.

C. Traditional techniques, medicine and calendars.

D. Traditional etiquette, festivals and other folk customs.

E. Traditional sports and entertainment.

2. Which of the following are intangible cultural heritage projects in Zhejiang Province?

A. Longquan Celadon Firing Technique.

B. Shuixiang Social Drama.

C. Yueqing Fine Grain Paper Cutting.

D. Painting.

3. What scenes does the Shuixiang Social Drama include?

A. Making a scene.

B. Caitou performance.

C. Mulian performance.

D. Tutou performance.

4. Which of the following are China's intangible cultural heritage projects?

A. Beijing Opera.

B. Tai chi.

C. Acupuncture.

D. The Spring Festival.

第二章　少数民族

（少数民族布艺装饰品　王晓慧供图）

第一课　少数民族简述

更多讲解，请扫码观看

中国共有 56 个民族，除了作为主体民族的汉族，共有 55 个少数民族。少数民族的人口占中国总人口的 8%—9%，人口较多的民族有壮族、维吾尔族、回族、苗族、满族、彝族、土家族等 18 个民族，人口均达到百万以上。而部分民族人口较少，比如有 6 个民族的人口在 1 万以下。55 个少数民族之中，壮族人口最多，高山族人口最少，而回族的分布最广。

中国的少数民族自治行政区划面积占全国总面积的 60% 以上，人口分布的特点为大杂居、小聚居，分布范围广，但主要集中在西部和边疆地区，以及西南、西北、东北等各省和自治区。其中内蒙古、新疆、西藏、广西、宁夏5个自治区，以及 30 个自治州、120 个自治县（旗）、1200 多个民族乡，都是少数民族的人民聚居的地方。

从风俗习惯上来说，在服装、饮食、居住、婚姻、礼仪、丧葬等方面，每个少数民族各具特色。少数民族的节日文化也丰富多样，比较有名的如蒙古族的那达慕大会、傣族的泼水节、傈僳族的刀杆节、彝族的火把节、白族的三月节、藏族的酥油花灯节、苗族的花山节等。

在民族政策上，中国坚持民族平等团结，实行民族区域自治，并鼓励和支持民族地区的经济和社会发展，重视推进少数民族的科学、教育、文化、卫生等事业，鼓励少数民族使用和发展其语言文字，尊重少数民族的风俗习惯，对少数民族的宗教信仰自由也予以尊重、保护。近年来，中国还实施了西部大开发战略，推行"兴边富民"等措施，并重点扶持人口较少的民族发展。

随着经济的发展，各民族之间的交流日益增多，各民族混居的现象将越来越普遍。少数民族人口在不断地从原聚居地区向全国各地区分散，但各少数民族仍保持本民族特色、传统文化和生活习俗等。

课堂思考与讨论

1. 了解中国少数民族的一些著名节日，并进行连线。

傣族   酥油花灯节

蒙古族   泼水节

彝族   那达慕大会

藏族   火把节

白族   花山节

苗族   三月节

2. 如果你的一个朋友对中国的少数民族文化感兴趣，请给他／她建议旅游的地方。

3. 你接触过中国的少数民族吗？你听说过或了解过某个民族的文化习俗吗？

4. 查找资料，了解你所感兴趣的某一个中国少数民族，以"图片＋文字"的方式进行介绍。

5. 你的国家或地区有哪些不同的民族？介绍不同民族之间的异同，或介绍某一个民族的特点。

6. 你如何看待不同民族之间的文化差异性？

A Brief Introduction of Ethnic Minorities

China has 56 ethnic groups, with a total of 55 ethnic minorities, except for the main ethnic group Han. The population of ethnic minorities accounts for 8% to 9% of the total population in China. Some groups have a larger population. There are 18 ethnic groups including the Zhuang, Uygur, Hui, Miao, Man, Yi, and Tujia with a population of over one million. There are six ethnic groups with a population of less than 10,000. Among the 55 ethnic minorities, the Zhuang ethnic group has the largest population, the Gaoshan ethnic group has the smallest population, and the Hui ethnic group has the widest distribution.

The area of minority autonomous administrative divisions of China accounts for more than 60% of the whole country. The ethnic groups generally choose to live among each other, while some live in concentrated communities of their own with a wide range of distribution. This is the characteristic of the distribution of minority populations. It is mainly concentrated in the western and border areas, provinces and autonomous regions in the southwest, northwest and northeast, of which five autonomous regions of Inner Mongolia, Xinjiang, Xizang, Guangxi and Ningxia, 30 autonomous prefectures, 120 autonomous counties (banners), and more than 1,200 ethnic townships are inhabited by ethnic minorities.

All ethnic minorities have unique customs, which are manifested in clothing, diet, residence, marriage, etiquette, funeral and other aspects. The festival culture is also rich and colorful, such as the Nadam Fair of the Mongolian, the Water-Splashing Festival of the Dai, the Knife-Ladder-Climbing Festival of the Lisu, the Torch Festival of the Yi, the March Festival of the Bai, the Butter Lantern Festival of the Zang, The Flower Mountain Festival of the Miao, etc.

China's ethnic policies mainly include adhering to ethnic equality and unity, regional ethnic autonomy, encouraging and supporting the economy and society development in ethnic minority areas, developing science, education, culture, health service and other undertakings of ethnic minorities, encouraging ethnic minorities to use and develop their own language, respecting ethnic minority customs and habits, respecting and protecting the freedom of religious belief of ethnic minorities. In recent years, China has also adopted the strategy to develop the western region, carried out measures such as "Revitalizing Border Areas and Enriching the People" and focused on supporting the development of ethnic groups with a smaller population.

With the development of the economy, communication between different ethnic groups increases day by day, and the phenomenon of mixed living among ethnic groups become more and more common. The population of ethnic minorities is continuing to spread from their original settlement areas to various regions across the country, but they still maintain their own ethnic characteristics, traditional culture, living customs and so on.

Think and discuss

1. Understand some famous festivals of ethnic minorities in China and try to link.

The Dai ethnic group   The Butter Lantern Festival

The Mongolian ethnic group   The Water-Splashing Festival

The Yi ethnic group   The Nadam Fair

The Zang ethnic group   The Torch Festival

The Bai ethnic group   The Flower Mountain Festival

The Miao ethnic group   The March Festival

2. If a friend of yours is interested in the culture of ethnic minorities in China, please suggest places to visit for him/her.

3. Have you ever contacted with ethnic minorities in China? Have you heard or learned the cultural customs of a certain ethnic group?

4. Search for information to learn about a certain Chinese ethnic minority that interests you and introduce it in the form of pictures and text.

5. What are the different ethnic groups in your country or region? Introduce the similarities and differences between different ethnic groups or introduce the characteristics of an ethnic group.

6. How do you view the cultural differences between different ethnic groups?

课后练习

一、判断题

1. 中国一共有 55 个民族。（　　　）

2. 苗族的人口最多。（　　　）

3. 在中国分布最广的少数民族是回族。（　　　）

4. 少数民族在中国分布的范围很广。（　　　）

5. 中国东南部是少数民族聚居的地区。（　　　）

6. 中国在民族政策上实行民族区域自治。（　　　）

二、单选题

1. 那达慕大会是_____的盛大节日。

A. 回族 　　　　　B. 壮族 　　　　　C. 蒙古族

2. 傣族比较有特色的节日是_____。

A. 三月节 　　　　B. 泼水节 　　　　C. 火把节

3. 少数民族人口约占中国总人口的_____。

A. 8%—9% 　　　 B. 18%—19% 　　　C. 60%

After-class exercises

I. True or false

1. There are 55 ethnic groups in China. (　　)

2. The Miao ethnic group has the largest population. (　　)

3. The most widely distributed ethnic minority in China is the Hui ethnic group. (　　)

4. Ethnic minorities are widely distributed in China. (　　)

5. The southeast of China is a major region inhabited by ethnic

minorities. (   )

6. China practices regional ethnic autonomy in its ethnic policy. (   )

II. Single choice

1. The Nadam Fair is a grand festival of _____.

A. the Hui ethnic group

B. the Zhuang ethnic group

C. the Mongolian ethnic group

2. One of the Dai ethnic group's distinctive festivals is _____.

A. the March Festival

B. the Water-Splashing Festival

C. the Torch Festival

3. Ethnic minority population accounts for about _____ of China's total population.

A. 8%–9%   B. 18%–19%   C. 60%

（浙江畲乡古城 王晓慧供图）

第二课 畲族三月三

更多讲解，请扫码观看

畲族是中国的一个少数民族，主要分布在福建、浙江、江西等地。根据《中国统计年鉴：2021》，畲族总人口为746385人。畲族有自己独特的文化和传统，其中最著名的就是畲族的婚姻文化和音乐文化。畲族是一个以水为生、依山而居的民族，主要从事水稻种植、渔猎和手工艺制作等传统职业。畲族社会的家族组织非常发达，以大家族为单位，重视家族祖先的崇拜和传承。畲族还有独特的语言，畲语属于汉藏语系的苗瑶语族。位于浙江丽水的景宁畲族自治县是中国唯一的畲族自治县，畲族人口占比约11%。

三月三是畲族重要的传统节日。它通常在中国农历三月初三这一天举行，是畲族人民祭祖、赏花、娱乐的盛大节日。在节日这天，畲族主要有以下活动：

赛龙舟：畲族人民会组织龙舟比赛活动，这是庆祝节日的重要活动之一。参赛组通常由 20 人组成，包括划手和鼓手，船上还会挂上五彩缤纷的旗帜和花环。

祭祖：畲族人民会前往祖先陵墓或祖庙，举行盛大的祭祖仪式，表达对祖先的崇敬之情，祈求祖先保佑子孙平安健康、五谷丰登。

赏花：畲族人民还会登山赏花。因此，畲族三月三也称花山节。在花山上，人们会聚集在一起，品尝畲族传统美食和特色小吃，如畲族糯米糍、红糖粿等，还会演唱畲乐和跳畲族舞蹈，增强节日气氛。

三月三是畲族传统文化中最重要的节日之一，具有悠久的历史和独特的文化内涵。这个节日不仅是畲族人民的重要文化遗产，也是中华民族多元文化的重要组成部分。近年来，中国政府高度重视少数民族的保护和发展，采取了一系列措施加强对少数民族地区的经济扶持和文化保护，努力促进少数民族地区的经济社会发展和文化传承。现在，畲族歌舞、服饰、语言、习俗、医药等传统文化传承和发展良好，畲族民歌、畲族三月三、畲族婚俗均被列入国家级非物质文化遗产代表性项目。

课堂思考与讨论

1. 畲族人口主要居住在哪些地方？

2. 三月三是畲族最重要的传统节日之一，它的主要活动有祭祖、唱歌跳舞、登山赏花。在你的国家有类似的传统节日吗？请介绍一下。

3. 除了畲族，中国还有哪些少数民族？

4. 你对畲族的哪个民俗活动最感兴趣？

5. 在你的国家，有没有类似的民俗活动？

The Sanyuesan Festival of the She Ethnic Group

The She ethnic group is a minority ethnic group in China, mainly distributed in Fujian, Zhejiang, Jiangxi and other places. The total population of the She ethnic group is 746,385, according to *China Statistical Yearbook: 2021*. The She ethnic group has its own unique culture and traditions, among which the most famous are the marriage culture and music culture of the She ethnic group. The She ethnic group is a nationality with people living by water and mountains, and mainly working in traditional occupations such as rice planting, fishing and hunting, and handicraft production. The family organization in the She ethnic society is very developed, with large families as the unit, attaching importance to the worship and inheritance of family ancestors. The She ethnic group also has its unique language. The She language belongs to the Miao-Yao branch of the Sino-Tibetan language family. Jingning She Autonomous County, located in Lishui, Zhejiang, is the only She autonomous county in China, with the She ethnic population accounting for approximately 11%.

The Sanyuesan Festival is an important traditional festival of the She ethnic group, usually held on the third day of the third lunar month. It is a grand festival for the She ethnic group to worship ancestors, appreciate flowers and entertain themselves. On the day of the Sanyuesan Festival, the She ethnic group mainly engages in the following activities:

Dragon boat races. The She people will organize dragon boat races, which is one of the important forms of celebration for the festival. The participating group usually consists of 20 people, including paddlers and drummers, and colorful flags and wreaths are also hung on the boat.

Ancestral worship activities. The She ethnic group will go to their ancestral tombs or temples to hold a grand ancestral worship ceremony, expressing their respect for their ancestors and praying to their ancestors for their safety, health, and good harvests.

Appreciating flowers. The She people will climb mountains and enjoy flowers. Therefore, the Sanyuesan Festival is also called the Huashan Festival. On the flower hills, People will gather together to taste the traditional food and special snacks, such as She glutinous rice, brown sugar rice, and sing She music and dance to enhance the festival atmosphere.

The Sanyuesan Festival is one of the most important festivals in the She traditional culture, with a long history and unique cultural connotation. This festival is not only an important cultural heritage of the She people, but also an important part of the multi-culture of the nation. In recent years, Chinese government attaches great importance to the protection and development of ethnic minorities, and has taken a series of measures to strengthen economic support and cultural protection of ethnic minority areas, and strives to promote the economic and social development and cultural inheritance of ethnic minority areas. At present, the traditional culture of the She, such as singing and dancing, clothing, language, customs, medicine, has been well inherited and developed. The She folk songs, the She Sanyuesan Festival, and the She marriage customs have been included in the national representative intangible cultural heritage.

 Think and discuss

1. Where does the She ethnic group mainly reside?

2. The Sanyuesan Festival is one of the most important traditional

festivals among the She ethnic group, with its main activities including ancestor worship, singing and dancing, and climbing mountains to appreciate flowers. Do you have similar traditional festivals in your country? Please introduce it.

3. Besides the She ethnic group, what other ethnic minorities are there in China?

4. Which folk activity of the She ethnic group are you most interested in?

5. Is there a similar folk activity in your country?

课后练习

一、填空题

1. 畲族是中国的一个少数民族，主要分布在福建、＿＿＿＿＿、江西等地。

2. 畲族有自己独特的文化和传统，其中最著名的就是畲族的_____和音乐文化。

3. 畲族是一个以水为生、依山而居的民族，主要从事_____、渔猎和手工艺制作等传统职业。

4. 位于_____的景宁畲族自治县是中国唯一的畲族自治县，畲族人口占比约 11%。

5. _____是畲族重要的传统节日，它通常在中国农历三月初三这一天举行，是畲族人民祭祖、赏花、娱乐的盛大节日。

6. 畲族三月三的主要活动有_____。

二、判断题

1. 畲族社会的家族组织非常发达，以大家族为单位，重视家族祖先的崇拜和传承。（　　　）

2. 畲族有自己的语言。（　　　）

3. 近年来，中国政府高度重视少数民族的保护和发展，采取了一系列措施加强对少数民族地区的经济扶持和文化保护，努力促进畲族等少数民族地区的经济社会发展和文化传承。（　　　）

4. 现在，畲族歌舞、服饰、语言、习俗、医药等传统文化传承和发展良好，畲族民歌、畲族三月三、畲族婚俗均被列入国家级非物质文化遗产代表性项目。（　　　）

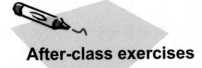

After-class exercises

I. Filling in the blanks

1. The She ethnic group is a minority ethnic group in China, mainly distributed in Fujian, _____ , Jiangxi, and other places.

2. The She ethnic group has its own unique culture and traditions, among which the most famous are the She ethnic group's _____ and music culture.

3. The She ethnic group is a nationality with people living by water and mountains, and mainly working in traditional occupations such as _____ , fishing and hunting, and handicraft production.

4. Jingning She Autonomous County located in _____ is the only She autonomous county in China, with the She population accounting for approximately 11%.

5. _____ is an important traditional festival of the She ethnic group, usually held on the third day of the third lunar month in China. It is a grand festival for the She ethnic group to worship ancestors, appreciate flowers, and entertain themselves.

6. The main activities of the Sanyuesan Festival are _____ .

II. True or false

1. The family organization in She society is very developed, with large families as the unit, emphasizing the worship and inheritance of family ancestors. (　　)

2. The She ethnic group has its own language. (　　)

3. In recent years, the Chinese government has attached great importance to the protection and development of ethnic minorities and has taken a series of measures to strengthen economic support and cultural protection of ethnic minority areas, striving to promote the economic and social development and cultural inheritance of ethnic minority areas. (　　)

4. Nowadays, the traditional culture of the She people, such as singing and dancing, clothing, language, customs, and medicine, has been well inherited and developed. The She folk songs, the Sanyuesan Festival, and the She marriage customs have all been included in the national representative intangible cultural heritage projects. (　　)

（文房四宝　吴雅云供图）

第一课　汉字与书法

汉字是中国最重要的书写符号，它是经过漫长历史发展形成的，起源可追溯至数千年前的古代中国。关于汉字的构造理论，有多种说法，其中最为流行的是"象形文字学说"和"指事文字学说"。汉代学者将汉字的构造和使用方式归纳为六种，总称"六书"。后世学者定名为象形、指事、会意、形声、转注、假借。

汉字是中国文化的重要组成部分，是中华文明的重要象征。汉字对中国文化的影响可以从多个方面来看。首先，汉字是中国文化的书写工具，为文化传承提供了重要的条件。很多重要的文化名著得以出现，如《论语》

更多讲解，请扫码观看

《道德经》《史记》等，这些文化经典对中国文化的形成和发展产生了深远的影响。其次，汉字本身也是中国文化的重要符号，很多重要的节日和文化活动都与汉字有关，它们代表着中国文化特有的精神和价值观。再次，汉字也是中国文化的艺术形式之一。书法、篆刻、印章等都是基于汉字的艺术形式，这些形式代表了中国文化的独特艺术风格，成为中国文化的重要表现形式。

中国书法的历史可以追溯到古代的甲骨文和金文时期，但正式形成并得到广泛发展是在汉代以后的魏晋南北朝时期。在这一时期，书法艺术开始呈现出多样化的形式和风格。在隋唐时期，书法艺术得到了极大的发展，形成了楷书、草书、行书、隶书、篆书等多种书法风格。其中，楷书具有清晰、端庄、秀美的特点，成为后世书法的标准形式。

课堂思考与讨论

1. 你认识"日""火""上""下""晴""睛"这几个汉字吗？你是怎么学习和记忆的？

2. 你体验或练习过书法吗？请介绍一下练习书法一般需要准备什么工具。

3. 很多中国人在春节的时候都会倒贴"福"字，这是为什么？

4. 你在你的国家见到过汉字吗？是在什么场合见到的？

5. 猜字谜：有一个字，上头小，下头大。这是什么字?

Chinese Characters and Calligraphy

Chinese characters are the most important written symbols, formed through a long history and can be traced back thousands of years to ancient China. There are many theories about the construction of Chinese characters, among which the most popular ones are the "pictographic writing theory" and the "indicative writing theory". Scholars in the Han Dynasty categorized the structure and use of Chinese characters into six types and collectively called "six writing ways". Later scholars named them pictographs, self-explanatory characters, associative compounds, pictophonetic characters, mutually explanatory characters and phonetic loan characters.

Chinese characters are an important component of Chinese culture and an important symbol of Chinese civilization. The influence of Chinese characters on Chinese culture can be seen from multiple aspects. Firstly, Chinese characters are the writing tool of Chinese culture, providing important conditions for the inheritance of culture. Many important cultural masterpieces emerged, such as *The Analects of Confucius*, the *Tao Te Ching*, and the *Records of the Grand Historian*, which had a profound impact on the formation and development of Chinese culture. Secondly,

Chinese characters are also important symbols of Chinese culture, and many important festivals and cultural activities are related to Chinese characters, representing the unique spirit and values of Chinese culture. Thirdly, Chinese characters are also one of the art forms of Chinese culture. Calligraphy, seal cutting, seals and other forms of art based on Chinese characters represent the unique art style of Chinese culture and have become important manifestations of Chinese culture.

The history of Chinese calligraphy can be traced back to the ancient oracle bone inscriptions and bronze inscriptions, but it was formally formed and widely developed in the Wei, Jin and Northern and Southern dynasties after the Han Dynasty. During this period, calligraphy art began to take on diverse forms and styles. During the Sui and the Tang dynasties, calligraphy art underwent great development, forming various calligraphy styles such as regular script, cursive script, running script, official script, and seal script. Among them, the regular script has the characteristics of clarity, dignity and beauty, becoming the standard form of calligraphy for later generations.

 Think and discuss

1. Do you know the Chinese characters "日" "火" "上" "下" "晴"

and "睛"? How do you learn and remember them?

2. Have you ever experienced or practiced calligraphy? What tools does it usually need to practice calligraphy?

3. Many Chinese people paste the character "福" upside down during the Spring Festival, why?

4. Have you ever seen Chinese characters in your country? On what occasion did you see them?

5. Game of guessing character: There is a character with a "小" top and a "大" bottom. What Chinese character is this?

课后练习

一、填空题

1. 关于汉字的构造理论，有多种说法，其中最为流行的是

"_____"和"指事文字学说"。

2. 汉代学者将汉字的构造和使用方式归纳为六种，总称"六书"。后世学者定名为_____、指事、会意、形声、转注、假借。

3. 中国书法的历史可以追溯到甲骨文和金文时期，但正式形成并得到广泛发展是在汉代以后的_____。

二、判断题

1. 汉字是中国文化的书写工具，为文化传承提供了重要的条件。（　　　）

2. 汉字本身也是中国文化的重要符号，很多重要的节日和文化活动都和汉字有关，它们代表着中国文化特有的精神和价值观。（　　　）

三、单选题

_____具有清晰、端庄、秀美的特点，成为后世书法的标准形式。

A. 楷书　　　　　B. 行书　　　　　C. 草书

四、多选题

_____等都是基于汉字的艺术形式，这些形式代表了中国文化的独特艺术风格，成为中国文化的重要表现形式。

A. 书法　　　　　B. 篆刻　　　　　C. 印章

After-class exercises

I. Filling in the blanks

1. There are many theories about the construction of Chinese characters, among which the most popular ones are the "_____" and the "indicative writing theory".

2. Scholars in the Han Dynasty categorized the structure and use of Chinese characters into six types and collectively called "six writing ways". Later scholars named them _____ , self-explanatory characters, associative compounds, pictophonetic characters, mutually explanatory characters and phonetic loan characters.

3. The history of Chinese calligraphy can be traced back to the ancient oracle bone inscriptions and bronze inscriptions, but its formal formation and widespread development occurred _____ after the Han Dynasty.

II. True or false

1. Chinese characters are the writing tool of Chinese culture, providing important conditions for cultural inheritance. (   )

2. Chinese characters are also important symbols of Chinese culture,

and many important festivals and cultural activities are related to Chinese characters, representing the unique spirit and values of Chinese culture. (   )

III. Single choice

_____ has the characteristics of clarity, dignity, and beauty, becoming the standard form of calligraphy in later generations.

A. Regular script   B. Running script   C. Cursive script

IV. Multiple choices

_____ etc. are all art forms based on Chinese characters, representing the unique art style of Chinese culture and becoming important manifestations of Chinese culture.

A. Calligraphy   B. Seal cutting   C. Seals

（浙江工商大学国际生练习书法   王晓华供图）

（绍兴兰亭　王晓慧供图）

第二课　绍兴酒与《兰亭序》

更多讲解，请扫码观看

　　绍兴酒，又称绍兴黄酒，在历史上曾有过各种名称，如山阴甜酒、越酿、花雕等，到了宋代才被称为"绍兴酒"。酿酒的匠人们通过摸索，将酒曲、鉴湖水、糯米融合酿出了一种具有独特风味的酒。酿酒工艺经过几千年的探索日臻完善成熟，整个酿酒过程要历经数十道工序，耗时 280 天，酿好以后，需保存在陶坛之中，再等上 3—5 年的时间，酒味才算成熟。绍兴酒呈琥珀色，香气浓郁，还富含氨基酸、脂类、微量醇和多种维生素，具有一定的营养价值。绍兴酒具有通气血、疏经络、养肤散湿等功效，如果适量饮用，有助于血液循环，促进体内新陈代谢。

绍兴酒历史悠久，其美味吸引了古今许多名人志士，他们饮酒助兴，饮酒作诗，留下许多美好的故事。东晋永和九年（公元353年），"书圣"王羲之与朋友在绍兴兰亭曲水流觞，吟诗写赋，写下的《兰亭序》流传至今。《兰亭序》被誉为中国最经典的行书作品之一，据说是王羲之在喝醉的时候创作而成的。

绍兴黄酒文化既是物质的，也是精神的；既可以高雅，也可以贴近平常人的生活。据说，越王勾践曾以绍兴酒作为奖励赏赐给生育儿女的人家，他也经常带着稻米和绍兴酒外出寻访人才。绍兴酒中，比较典型的是"女儿红"和"状元红"。在古代绍兴，如果家里有孩子出生，家里就会酿造几十罐好酒，然后邀请工匠在酒坛子上雕刻和绘制精美的图案，并将其密封存放在桂花树下。如果生的是女孩，这种酒就叫"女儿红"，如果生的是男孩，这种酒就叫"状元红"。时至今日，在绍兴和其他部分江南地区的一些人家，仍保留着酿造"女儿红"和"状元红"的习俗。

 课堂思考与讨论

1. 绍兴酒是一种什么酒？跟葡萄酒有什么区别？

2. 你了解中国酒的类别吗？你尝过或听说过哪些中国特色酒？

3. 你的国家有没有著名的特色酒类？试着将其与绍兴酒进行简单的比较。

4. 在你的国家一般哪些人喝酒？人们在什么时候或什么场合喝酒？

5. 饮酒与人们的生活有什么特别的联系吗？试着将你国家的酒文化与中国酒文化进行比较。

Shaoxing Wine and the *Lanting Xu*

Shaoxing wine, also known as Shaoxing rice wine, had a variety of names in history, such as Shanyin sweet wine, Yue wine and Huadiao, and it was not called "Shaoxing wine" until the Song Dynasty. The makers of wine went through a long period of exploration, and found a way of mixing the distiller's yeast, water from Jianhu Lake, and glutinous rice to brew a unique flavor of wine. Winemaking technique after thousands of years of exploration is becoming perfect and mature.The whole process goes through dozens of processes, taking 280 days, and after brewing, the wine needs to be preserved in the pottery jar, and after three to five years, the wine is mature. Shaoxing wine is in amber with rich aroma. It's rich in amino acids, lipids, a trace of alcohol and a variety of vitamins, and it is said to have some nutritional value. Shaoxing wine has the effect of improving the circulation of vital energy (qi) and blood, dredging meridians and collaterals, nourishing skin and dispelling dampness. An appropriate amount of drinking may help blood circulation and promote metabolism in the body.

Shaoxing wine has a long history, and its deliciousness has attracted many celebrities of ancient and modern times. They drank to cheer, drank to write poems, and left many beautiful stories. In the 9th year of Yonghe in the Eastern Jin Dynasty (353 AD), Wang Xizhi, the "sage of the calligraphy", once drank wine and wrote poems with friends in the Lanting (Orchid Pavilion) in Shaoxing, and wrote the *Lanting Xu* (literally "preface to poems composed at the orchid pavilion"), which has been handed down to this day and is known as one of the most classic Chinese calligraphy works. It is said that Wang Xizhi wrote it when he was drunk.

Shaoxing rice wine culture is both material and spiritual. It is said that King Gou Jian of the State of Yue once gave Shaoxing wine as a prize to the family that gave birth to children, and he often went out to seek talents with rice and Shaoxing wine. In Shaoxing wine, the more typical types are "Nu'er Hong" (Daughter Red) and "Zhuangyuan Hong" (Scholar Red). In ancient Shaoxing, if a child was born in the family, the family would brew dozens of jars of fine wine, and then invite artisans to carve and paint exquisite patterns on the wine jars and store them sealed under the osmanthus tree. If the baby is a girl, this wine is called "Nu'er Hong", and if the baby is a boy, this wine is called "Zhuangyuan Hong". Today, some families in Shaoxing and other parts of the Jiangnan region still retain the custom of brewing

Nu'er Hong and Zhuangyuan Hong.

Think and discuss

1. What is Shaoxing wine? What is the difference between it and grape wine?

2. Do you know the categories of Chinese liquor? What Chinese local special wines have you tasted or heard of?

3. Do you have any famous special alcoholic beverage in your country? Try to make a simple comparison between it and Shaoxing wine.

4. Who generally drinks in your country, and when or on what occasions do people drink?

5. Is there any special connection between drinking alcohol and people's lives? Try to compare your country's wine culture with Chinese wine culture.

课后练习

一、判断题

1. 从酒的分类上看，绍兴酒是一种黄酒。（　　　）

2. 绍兴酒有营养价值，多喝对身体好。（　　　）

3. 王羲之的《兰亭序》是在绍兴完成的。（　　　）

4. 绍兴酒是用葡萄酿造的。（　　　）

5. 中国古代的名人志士也很喜欢绍兴酒。（　　　）

6. 绍兴酒太贵，普通的家庭不喝绍兴酒。（　　　）

7. 绍兴酒有很长的历史。（　　　）

二、单选题

1. 《兰亭序》是中国经典的_____。

A. 书法作品　　　B. 绘画作品　　　C. 建筑作品

2. 如果一户家庭出生的孩子是个女孩，她家人为她保存的酒叫作_____。

A. 状元红　　　　B. 女儿红　　　　C. 花雕

3. 绍兴酒一般是什么颜色的？

A. 白色   B. 黄色   C. 琥珀色

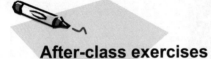

After-class exercises

I. True or false

1. From the perspective of wine classification, Shaoxing wine is a kind of rice wine. (   )

2. Shaoxing wine has nutritional value, and drinking more is good for health. (   )

3. The *Langting Xu* by Wang Xizhi was completed in Shaoxing. (   )

4. Shaoxing wine is made from grapes. (   )

5. Shaoxing wine was also loved by famous people in ancient China. (   )

6. Shaoxing wine is too expensive, and ordinary families do not drink it. (   )

7. Shaoxing wine has a long history. (   )

II. Single choice

1. The *Langting Xu* is a Chinese classic_____.

A. calligraphy work　　　B. painting work　　　C. architectural work

2. If a family gives birth to a girl, the wine they save for her is called _____.

A. Zhuangyuan Hong　　　B. Nu'er Hong　　　C. Huadiao

3. What color is Shaoxing wine usually?

A. White.　　　　　　B. Yellow.　　　　　C. Amber.

（装饰绍兴酒坛　王晓慧供图）

话题三　感知中国社会

● 第一章　五彩中国

● 第二章　百姓日常

● 第三章　教育科技

（四川九寨沟瀑布　王晓慧供图）

第一章　五彩中国

第一课　中国的世界遗产

更多讲解，请扫码观看

　　从 1986 年到 2024 年，中国共有 59 项世界文化和自然遗产被列入世界遗产名录，中国目前是世界遗产种类最齐全、世界自然遗产数量最多的国家之一。中国的世界遗产分布在 29 个省、自治区、直辖市和特别行政区，北京是世界上拥有遗产数量（8 项）最多的城市。

　　中国的世界文化遗产共 40 项，包括长城、紫禁城、莫高窟、秦始皇陵及兵马俑坑、周口店北京人遗址、山东孔府、西藏布达拉宫、武当山古建筑群、丽江古城等。作为世界文化遗产的苏州园林，集中了江南园林建筑的精华，代表了不同时期的建筑风格，在世界园林发展史上占有重要地位；布达拉宫是中国著名的藏传佛教寺庙，是宗教、艺术和文化的宝库。中国的 6 项世界文化景观为江西庐山风景名胜区、山西五台山、杭州西湖文化景观、云南红河哈尼梯田、广西左江花山岩画、普洱景迈山古茶林文化景观。杭州西湖文化景观包含了西湖自然山水风光、城湖空间特征、西湖十大景区等独特元素，是中国景观美学理念的体现，也是自然美与人文美的完美结合。普洱景迈山古茶林文化景观于 2023 年 9 月被列入世界遗产名录，是全球首个茶主题世界文化遗产。

中国的世界自然遗产共 15 项，包括四川黄龙国家级名胜区、四川九寨沟国家级名胜区、湖南武陵源国家级名胜区、云南"三江并流"自然景观、四川大熊猫栖息地、中国南方喀斯特、江西三清山风景名胜区、中国丹霞、湖北神农架、青海可可西里等，其中四川大熊猫栖息地是世界上最大、最完整的大熊猫栖息地。中国的 4 项世界文化和自然遗产包括山东泰山、安徽黄山、四川峨眉山—乐山大佛、福建武夷山，山中的文化杰作与自然景观完美结合。

课堂思考与讨论

1. 根据图片选择对应的景点名称。

A

B

C

D

杭州西湖（　　）　　　　　　北京故宫（　　）

西安秦始皇兵马俑（　　）　　四川九寨沟（　　）

2. 在中国，你曾经去过哪些被列入世界遗产名录的景点？谈谈你的旅游感受。如果你还没去过任何一处景点，请查资料说说你最想去的几个地方。

3. 你所在的国家有哪些被列入世界遗产名录的景点？请使用图片和简单的文字进行介绍。

4. 如果你是一名导游，能否设计一份在中国三日游或七日游的行程安排？

Chinese World Heritage Sites

From 1986 to 2024, a total of 59 World Cultural and Natural Heritage Sites in China were inscribed on the World Heritage List, making China one of the countries with the most complete variety of World Heritage and the largest number of World Natural Heritage Sites. China's World Heritage Sites are distributed in 29 provinces, autonomous regions, municipalities directly under the Central Government and special administrative regions, and Beijing has the largest number of heritage sites (8) in the world.

According to the classification, there are 40 World Cultural Heritage Sites, including the Great Wall, the Forbidden City, the Mogao Grottoes, the Tomb of the First Emperor of the Qin, the "Peking Man" site in Zhoukoudian, Temple and Cemetery of Confucius and the Kong Family Mansion in Qufu, Shandong, the Potala Palace in Xizang, the Ancient Building Complex in the Wudang Mountains, the Old Town of Lijiang and so on. As a World Cultural Heritage, Suzhou Gardens concentrate the essence

of garden architecture in the south of the Yangtze River, representing the architectural styles of different periods, and occupy an important position in the history of world garden development. Potala Palace is a famous Tibetan Buddhism temple of Xizang in China and a treasure house of religion, art and culture. The six World Cultural Landscapes in China are the Jiangxi Lushan Scenic Area, the Shanxi Wutai Mountain, the Hangzhou West Lake Cultural Landscape, the Yunnan Honghe Hani Terraces, the Guangxi Zuojiang Huashan Rock Paintings and the Pu'er Jingmai Mountain Ancient Tea Forest Cultural Landscape. The Hangzhou West Lake Cultural Landscape contains unique elements such as the natural landscape scenery of the West Lake, the spatial characteristics of the city lake, and the ten scenic spots of the West Lake, which is the embodiment of the concept of Chinese landscape aesthetics and the perfect combination of natural beauty and the beauty of humanism. The Pu'er Jingmai Mountain Ancient Tea Forest Cultural Landscape was inscribed on the world Heritage List in September 2023 and is the world's first tea-themed world cultural heritage.

There are 15 World Natural Heritage Sites, including the Sichuan Huanglong National Scenic Area, the Sichuan Jiuzhaigou National Scenic Area, the Hunan Wulingyuan National Scenic Area, the Yunnan "Three Parallel Rivers" Natural Landscape, the Sichuan Giant Panda Sanctuaries, the South China Karst, Jiangxi Sanqingshan Scenic Area, China Danxia, Hubei Shennongjia, Qinghai Hoh Xili, etc., among which the Sichuan Giant Panda Sanctuaries are the largest and most complete panda habitat in the world. China's four World Cultural and Natural Heritage Sites include Shandong Mount Taishan, Anhui Mount Huangshan, Sichuan Mount Emei Scenic Area, including Leshan Giant

Buddha Scenic Area, and Fujian Mount Wuyi, where cultural masterpieces in the mountains combine perfectly with natural landscapes.

Think and discuss

1. Select the corresponding name of the scenic spot based on the image.

A

B

C

D

West Lake, Hangzhou（　　）　　Forbidden City, Beijing（　　）

Terracotta Warriors, Xi'an（　　）Jiuzhaigou, Sichuan（　　）

2. What scenic areas in China have you ever been to on the World Heritage List? Talk about your travel experiences. If you haven't been to any tourist attractions yet, please check the information and list the places you want to visit the most.

3. What scenic areas are included in the World Heritage List in your country? Please use pictures and brief text to introduce them.

4. If you are a tour guide, can you design a travel plan for a three-day or seven-day tour in China?

课后练习

一、判断题

1. 中国目前是世界自然遗产数量最多的国家。（   ）

2. 庐山和五台山属于世界自然遗产。（   ）

3. 山东孔府属于世界文化遗产。（　　　）

二、单选题

1. 中国共有_____项世界文化和自然遗产。

A. 55　　　　　　B. 59　　　　　　C. 67

2. _____有8项世界遗产，是世界上拥有遗产数量最多的城市。

A. 北京　　　　　B. 杭州　　　　　C. 西安

3. 世界上第一个茶主题世界文化遗产是_____。

A. 杭州龙井茶园

B. 普洱景迈山古茶林文化景观

C. 福建武夷山岩茶茶园

4. _____集中了江南园林建筑精华，是世界文化遗产。

A. 苏州园林　　　B. 故宫　　　　　C. 杭州西湖

5. 四川有名的世界自然遗产是_____。

A. 黄山　　　　　B. 三清山　　　　C. 大熊猫栖息地

6. 世界文化和自然遗产是文化杰作与自然景观的完美结合，比如_____。

A. 泰山　　　　　B. 长城　　　　　C. 布达拉宫

7. 杭州的西湖属于_____。

A. 世界自然遗产　B. 世界文化景观　C. 世界文化和自然遗产

After-class exercises

I. True or false

1. China currently has the largest number of World Natural Heritage Sites. (   )

2. Mount Lushan and Mount Wutai are World Natural Heritage Sites. (   )

3. Temple and Cemetery of Confucius and the Kong Family Mansion in Qufu, Shandong Province is a World Cultural Heritage Site. (   )

II. Single choice

1. China shares _____ World Cultural and Natural Heritage Sites.

A. 55   B. 59   C. 67

2. (   ) has 8 World Heritage Sites, and it is the city with the largest number of heritage sites in the world.

A. Beijing   B. Hangzhou   C. Xi'an

3. The world's first tea-themed World Cultural Heritage site is _____.

A. Hangzhou Longjing Tea Garden

B. Pu'er Jingmai Mountain Ancient Tea Forest Cultural Landscape

C. Fujian Wuyishan Rock Tea Garden

4. _____ gather the essence of Jiangnan garden architecture. It is the World Cultural Heritage.

A. Suzhou Gardens　B. The Imperial Palace　　C. Hangzhou West Lake

5. Sichuan's famous World Natural Heritage Site is _____.

A. Mount Huangshan　B. Sanqingshan Scenic Area　C. Giant Panda Sanctuaries

6. World Cultural and Natural Heritage is the perfect combination of cultural masterpieces and natural landscapes, such as _____.

A. Mount Taishan　　B. The Great Wall　　　C. The Potala Palace

7. Hangzhou West Lake is included on the list of _____.

A. World Natural Heritage

B. World Cultural Landscape

C. World Cultural and Natural Heritage

（西湖初秋　王晓慧供图）

（浙江丽水云和梯田　王晓慧供图）

第二课　浙江风采

更多讲解，请扫码观看

　　浙江省位于中国东南沿海，东临东海，与福建、江西、安徽、上海、江苏等省市接壤。浙江省属于亚热带海洋性气候，气候温和，四季分明，雨量充沛，水利资源丰富，钱塘江是最大的河流。夏季多雨，冬季湿润，春秋两季气候宜人，适合旅游和居住。

　　在古代，浙江是中国南方的一个重要经济文化中心。浙江的地理位置优越，加上经济繁荣，使得浙江成为古代海上丝绸之路和南方陆上丝绸之路的交会点，也是中国东南沿海对外交流的重要窗口。

　　近年来，浙江省的经济发展一直保持较快的增长势头，已经成为中国经济的重要增长点之一。首先，浙江省的制造业非常发达，涵盖了许多不同的产业，如纺织、轻工、机械、电子、汽车等。其次，浙江省的服务业也非常发达，在金融、旅游、物流等领域都有着强大的竞争力。杭州作为中国的互联网金融中心之一，吸引了大量的金融机构和人才聚集。此外，浙江的旅游业也十分繁荣，拥有众多的名胜古迹和自然风光，吸引了大量的国内外游客。杭州西湖、嘉兴南湖、安吉竹海、桐乡乌镇、义乌市场、舟山普陀山、金华横店影视城等都是浙江著名的旅游胜地。最后，浙江省十分注重创新和科技发展，拥有多所高水平的大学和研究机构，如浙江大学、宁波大学、中国美术学院、浙江工业大学、浙江工商大学等。浙江省政府出台了多项政策，鼓励企业加大研发投入，推动科技创新和产业升级。

　　截至 2023 年底，浙江省常住人口 6627 万人，是中国人口大省之一。浙江人口密度较高，主要聚集在杭州、宁波、温州、金华等城市和沿海地区。总体来说，浙江省的经济发展非常活跃和多元化，不仅在制造业、服务业等传统领域有着较强的竞争力，而且在新兴产业和科技领域不断迭代和创新，为中国的经济发展做出了重要贡献。

课堂思考与讨论

1. 在地图上找到中国浙江，看一看它的地理位置。

2. 用一个词概括你对浙江的了解或印象。

3. 分享一张你在浙江旅行时的照片，并用一句话介绍它。

4. "浙江"这一名称和浙江省的母亲河有关，你知道这条河的名字吗？

5. 请介绍一下你的大学所在的省份和城市。

The Charm of Zhejiang

Zhejiang Province is located in the southeast coast of China, bordering the East China Sea to the east. It borders city and provinces including Fujian, Jiangxi, Anhui, Shanghai, and Jiangsu. Zhejiang Province has a subtropical oceanic climate with mild climate, four distinct seasons and abundant rainfall. Zhejiang is rich in water resources, and the Qiantang River is the largest river. Summer is rainy, and winter is humid, and the climate in spring and autumn is pleasant, making it suitable for tourism and living.

In ancient times, Zhejiang was an important political, economic, and cultural center in southern China. With its superior geographical location and prosperous economy, Zhejiang has become the intersection of the ancient Maritime Silk Road and the Southern Land Silk Road, and also an important window for foreign exchanges in China's southeast coast.

In recent years, the economic development of Zhejiang Province has maintained a rapid growth momentum and has become one of the important growth points of China's economy. Firstly, the manufacturing industry in Zhejiang Province is very developed, covering many different industries, such as textiles, light industry, machinery, electronics, automobiles. Secondly, the service industry in Zhejiang Province is also very developed, such as finance, tourism, logistics and other fields, all of which have strong competitiveness. As one of China's internet finance centers, Hangzhou has attracted a large number of financial institutions and talents gathering. Zhejiang's tourism industry is also very prosperous, with numerous scenic spots and natural scenery, attracting a large number of domestic and foreign tourists. Hangzhou West Lake, Jiaxing South Lake, Anji Bamboo Sea, Tongxiang Wuzhen, Yiwu Market, Zhoushan Putuo Mountain, Jinhua Hengdian Film and Television City are all famous tourist destinations in Zhejiang. Finally, Zhejiang Province also attaches great importance to innovation and scientific and technological development, and has many high-level universities and research institutions, such as Zhejiang University, Ningbo University, China Academy of Art, Zhejiang University of Technology, Zhejiang Gongshang University and so on. The Zhejiang

Provincial Government has also introduced multiple policies to encourage enterprises to increase research and development investment, promote technological innovation and industrial upgrading.

As of the end of 2023, the permanent population of Zhejiang Province was 66.27 million, making it one of the most populous provinces in China. Zhejiang has a high population density, with populations concentrated in cities such as Hangzhou, Ningbo, Wenzhou, Jinhua, and coastal areas. Overall, the economic development of Zhejiang Province is very active and diversified. It not only has strong competitiveness in traditional fields such as manufacturing and service industries, but also continuously iterates and innovates in emerging industries and technology fields, making important contributions to China's economic development.

 Think and discuss

1. Find Zhejiang on the map, and take a look at its geographical location.

2. Summarize your impression of Zhejiang in one word.

3. Share a photo of yourself while traveling in Zhejiang and introduce it in one sentence.

4. The name "Zhejiang" is related to the mother river in Zhejiang Province. Do you know the name of this river?

5. Please introduce the province and city where your university is located.

一、单选题

1. 浙江省位于中国东南沿海，东临东海，省内最大河流是_____。

A. 黄河　　　　　B. 长江　　　　　C. 钱塘江

2. 下面哪一个省或者市不与浙江接壤？

A. 北京　　　　　B. 上海　　　　　C. 江苏

二、多选题

1. 浙江省的制造业非常发达，涵盖了许多不同的产业，如_____、电子、汽车等。

A. 纺织　　　　　B. 轻工　　　　　C. 机械

2. 浙江省的服务业也非常发达，在_____等领域都有着强大的竞争力。

A. 金融　　　　　B. 旅游　　　　　C. 物流

3. 下面哪些旅游胜地在浙江省？

A. 杭州西湖　　　B. 桐乡乌镇　　　C. 舟山普陀山

4. 浙江人口密度较高，主要聚集在_____、金华等城市和沿海地区。

A. 杭州　　　　　B. 宁波　　　　　C. 温州

三、判断题

1. 浙江省十分注重创新和科技发展，拥有多所高水平的大学和研究机构。浙江省政府出台了多项政策，鼓励企业加大研发投入，推动科技创新和产业升级。（　　　）

2. 浙江省属于亚热带海洋性气候，气候温和，四季分明，适合旅游和居住。（　　　）

After-class exercises

I. Single choice

1. Zhejiang Province is located on the southeast coast of China, adjacent to the East China Sea to the east. The largest river in its territory is _____.

   A. Yellow River   B. Yangtze River   C. Qiantang River

2. Which province or city below does not border Zhejiang?

   A. Beijing.   B. Shanghai.   C. Jiangsu.

II. Multiple choices

1. The manufacturing industry in Zhejiang Province is very developed, covering many different industries, such as _____, electronics, automobiles, etc.

   A. textiles   B. light industry   C. machinery

2. The service industry in Zhejiang Province is also very developed, with strong competitiveness in fields such as _____.

   A. finance   B. tourism   C. logistics

3. Which tourist destinations are in Zhejiang Province?

   A. Hangzhou West Lake.

B. Tongxiang Wuzhen.

C. Zhoushan Putuo Mountain.

4. Zhejiang has a high population density, with populations concentrated in cities such as _____, Jinhua, and coastal areas.

A. Hangzhou   B. Ningbo   C. Wenzhou

III. True or false

1. Zhejiang Province places great emphasis on innovation and technological development, with multiple high-level universities and research institutions. The Zhejiang Provincial Government has also introduced multiple policies to encourage enterprises to increase research and development investment, promote technological innovation and industrial upgrading. (   )

2. Zhejiang Province belongs to a subtropical marine climate with a mild climate and distinct four seasons, making it suitable for tourism and living. (   )

第二章　百姓日常

（鸳鸯火锅　谌曾灵供图）

第一课　中华美食

更多讲解，请扫码观看

中华美食，博大精深，源远流长。中华美食，看的是色，闻的是香，吃的是味，听的是故事。中国有八大菜系，分别为鲁（山东地区）菜（例如：葱烧海参）、川（四川地区）菜（例如：麻婆豆腐）、粤（广东地区）菜（例如：蜜汁叉烧）、苏（江苏地区）菜（例如：红烧狮子头）、闽（福建地区）菜（例如：佛跳墙）、浙（浙江地区）菜（例如：龙井虾仁）、湘（湖南地区）菜（例如：剁椒鱼头）、徽（安徽地区）菜（例如：火腿炖甲鱼）。中国饮食文化的菜系，指的是在一个特定地区内，由于气候、地理环境、历史背景、自然资源以及饮食习俗的差异，经过长期的历史发展而形成的一系列独特的烹饪技巧和口味，并且得到了全国范围内的认可。早在商周时期，中国的饮食文化就已经初露端倪，以姜子牙为代表。到了春秋战国时期的齐桓公时代，饮食文化中的南北菜肴风格已经开始显现出差异。到了唐宋时期，南方和北方的饮食风格各自形成了独立的体系。在南宋时期，中国的南北口味差异开始显现，形成了南方偏好甜食而北方偏好咸食的局面。随着时间的推移，到清朝初期，四川、山东、江苏、广东等地的菜肴逐渐崛起，它们被称为四大地方菜系，对当时的饮食文化产生了深远的影响。然而，在清朝末期，浙江、福建、湖南、安徽等地的新兴菜系也开始崭露头角，这四种新的地方菜系与原有的四大菜系一起构成了汉民族饮食文化的"八大菜系"。

同时，中国民间各具特色的地方名菜深受百姓喜爱。例如北京烤鸭、天津狗不理包子、云南过桥米线、常熟叫花鸡、杭州西湖醋鱼等，几乎每一款名吃，背后都有一个令人回味无穷的故事，这就是中华美食的魅力所在。中国中央电视台特别制作了一部关于美食的纪录片《舌尖上的中国》，将具体人物和故事串联，讲述了中国各地的美食生态。该纪录片风靡全球。

在中国还有一种节庆美食，贯穿每一个中华传统节日，为节日送上味觉盛宴。人们会在春节吃饺子，在元宵节吃汤圆，在中秋节吃月饼，在清明节吃青团，在端午节吃粽子，每一个节日美食都有着悠久的历史，记录了中国历史上的名人事迹和风俗习惯。

课堂思考与讨论

1. 你在中国最喜欢的美食是什么？请和大家分享你的中华美食故事。

2. 中外学生讨论：你的国家有什么代表性的美食？请介绍一个最具代表性的美食。

3. 中国八大菜系，你最喜欢哪一个菜系？请说出你的理由。

4. 从网络上搜索一个中国名菜的烹饪视频，在课堂上和同学交流分享。

Chinese Cuisine

Chinese cuisine is vast and profound, with a long history. For Chinese cuisine, people see color, enjoy fragrance, taste flavour, and listen to stories. There are eight major cuisines in China, namely Shandong cuisine (e.g. Braised Sea Cucumber with Scallion), Sichuan cuisine (e.g. Mapo Tofu), Guangdong cuisine (e.g. Honey-Stewed BBQ Pork), Jiangsu cuisine (e.g. Braised Pork Ball in Brown Sauce), Fujian cuisine (e.g. Fotiaoqiang, steamed abalone with sharks' fin and fish maw in broth), Zhejiang cuisine (e.g. Fried Shrimps with Longjing Tea), Hunan cuisine (e.g. Steamed Fish Head with Diced Hot Red Peppers), and Anhui cuisine (e.g. Braised

Turtle with Ham). The cuisine of Chinese culinary culture refers to a set of self-contained cooking techniques and flavors that have evolved over a long period of time due to differences in climate, terrain, history, natural resources, and dietary customs within a certain region, and are recognized throughout the country as local dishes. As early as the Shang and the Zhou dynasties, Chinese dietary culture had already taken shape, with Jiang Ziya being the most representative. Later, during the Spring and Autumn and Warring States periods of Qi Huangong, there were differences in the flavors of northern and southern dishes in dietary culture. By the Tang and the Song dynasties, the southern and northern regions had formed their own systems. During the Southern Song Dynasty, taste differences between the north and the south of China began to appear, forming a situation in which the south preferred sweets while the north preferred salty food. In the early years of the Qing Dynasty, Sichuan cuisine, Shandong cuisine, Huaiyang cuisine, and Guangdong cuisine became the most influential local cuisines at that time and were called the four major regional cuisines. By the end of the Qing Dynasty, four new regional cuisines, namely Zhejiang cuisine, Fujian cuisine, Hunan cuisine and Anhui cuisine, had been formed, which together with the original four cuisines constituted the "eight major cuisines" of the Han dietary culture.

At the same time, there are also distinctive local delicacies among the Chinese people, which are deeply loved by the people. For example, Beijing Roast Duck, Tianjin Goubuli Steamed Bun, Yunnan Rice Noodles,

Changshu Beggar's Chicken, Hangzhou West Lake Fish in Vinegar Sauce, and so on, almost every famous food has a memorable story behind it, which is the charm of Chinese food. China Central Television has specially produced a documentary about food called *A Bite of China*, which connects specific characters and stories, and tells the food ecology of various parts of China. This documentary has become popular worldwide.

In China, there is also a type of festive cuisine that runs through every traditional Chinese festival, providing a taste feast for the festival. People will eat dumplings during the Spring Festival and tangyuan (Glutinous rice balls) during the Lantern Festival, eat moon cakes on the Mid-Autumn Festival, eat qingtuan or green dumplings on the Tomb-Sweeping Festival, and eat zongzi on the Dragon Boat Festival. Each festival food has a long history, recording the deeds of celebrities and customs in Chinese history.

 Think and discuss

1. What is your favorite food in China? Please share your story of Chinese cuisine with everyone.

2. Chinese and foreign students' discussion: What are the representative cuisines in your country? Please introduce the most representative cuisine.

3. Which of the eight major Chinese cuisines do you like best? Please provide your reasons.

4. Search for a cooking video of a famous Chinese dish online and share it with classmates in the class.

课后练习

一、填空题

1. 中国有八大菜系，分别为_____菜、_____菜、_____菜、_____菜、_____菜、_____菜、_____菜、_____菜。

2. 中国的节庆美食有_____（请列举 3 个）。

3. 中国民间还有各具特色的地方名吃，比如_____（请列举 3 个）。

4. 在中秋节，人们吃_____赏月。

5. 在端午节，人们吃_____来纪念爱国诗人屈原。

二、判断题

1. 川菜是中国八大菜系之一。（　　　）

2. 到了南宋时期，北甜南咸的饮食风格形成。（　　　）

3. 中国中央电视台制作的美食纪录片叫《舌尖上的祖国》。（　　　）

4. 中国饮食文化的菜系，是指在一定区域内，由于气候、地形、历史、物产及饮食风俗的不同，经过漫长历史演变而形成的一整套自成体系的烹饪技艺和风味，但不被全国各地所承认的地方菜肴。（　　　）

5. 西湖醋鱼是杭州的地方名菜。（　　　）

After-class exercises

I. Filling in the blanks

1. There are eight major cuisines in China, which are _____ , _____ , _____ , _____ , _____ , _____ , _____ , and _____ .

2. Chinese festival food includes _____ (please list three).

3. Chinese folk also have their own unique local famous food, such as _____ (please list three).

4. On the Mid-Autumn Festival, people eat _____ and admire the moon.

5. On the Dragon Boat Festival, people eat _____ to commemorate the patriotic poet Qu Yuan.

II. True or false

1. Sichuan cuisine is one of the eight major cuisines in China. (   )

2. In the Southern Song Dynasty, the eating style of sweet in the north and salty in the south was formed. (   )

3. The food documentary produced by China Central Television is called *Motherland on the Tongue*. (   )

4. The cuisine of Chinese culinary culture refers to a set of self-contained cooking techniques and flavors that have evolved over a long period of time due to differences in climate, terrain, history, products, and dietary customs within a certain region, and are not recognized throughout the country as local dishes. (   )

5. West Lake Fish in Sweet and Sour Sauce is a famous local dish in Hangzhou. (   )

（湖州高铁　许飞燕供图）

第二课　高铁去湖州

更多讲解，请扫码观看

中国的高速铁路从起步到发展，再到全球领先，走出了一条独具特色的创新之路。从 20 世纪 90 年代开始，中国集中科研力量展开广泛深入的研究。经过多年努力，中国高铁已达到运营里程世界最长、商业运营速度世界最快、运营网络通达度世界最高的顶尖水平。中国铁路先后破解了青藏铁路、川藏铁路建设等技术难题。随着信息化时代的

143

到来，中国高铁实现了高铁网与互联网"双网融合"，推出了电子客票、移动支付、在线选座、刷脸进站、网上订餐等服务，满足了人们更多的出行体验。

高铁湖州站于 2013 年 7 月 1 日正式投入使用，总建筑面积 19920 平方米，站房主体设计如同一只白鹭展翅，象征湖州经济的飞跃。合杭高铁湖杭段开通以后，湖州铁路枢纽发展更加通畅，"轨道上的湖州"加速驶来。湖杭段成为浙江铁路网的一条重要连接线，将助推长三角城际铁路网的建设，全面构建浙江 1 小时交通圈。合杭高铁湖杭段跨越了湖州和杭州许多地区，人们坐上这趟列车，既能欣赏湖州的风景，又能欣赏杭州的富春江，可谓美不胜收。

高铁的快速建设带动了浙江湖州的经济发展。湖州自古以"丝绸之府"享誉海内外。从钱山漾出土的丝片来看，湖州丝绸已有 4700 多年的历史。湖州是迄今为止种桑养蚕、缫丝织造的发祥地之一。2015 年被命名为"世界丝绸之源"。近年来，随着丝绸产业的转型升级，湖州已形成从种桑养蚕、缫丝织绸、印染整理到终端产品出口的完整产业链。"世界丝绸之源"乘着中国高铁的东风开启了"新丝路"，把更多优质的丝织产品销往世界各地。

湖州也有许多美食，其中莫干笋、阁老毛腌鸡、湖州大馄饨、诸老大粽子、新市羊肉、德清青虾、钟管老鸭煲、太湖四珍、雷甸西瓜、太湖鹅等都是当地的特色美食。湖笔，与徽墨、宣纸、端砚并称为"文房四宝"，是悠久灿烂的中华文明的重要象征。

课堂思考与讨论

1. 制订一个乘坐高铁的出行计划，体验中国高铁的速度与服务。

2. 比较一下乘坐高铁和其他交通工具出行的优缺点。

3. 中国出口的商品，通过铁路运输能送达哪些国家？

4. 浙江湖州有哪些特产？

5. 除了中国，还有哪些国家也生产丝绸？

Taking High-Speed Railway to Huzhou

China's high-speed railway has embarked on a unique path of innovation from its inception, development, and global leadership. Since the 1990s, China has concentrated its research efforts to conduct extensive and in-depth research. After years of hard work, China's high-speed rail has reached the world's longest operating mileage, fastest commercial operation speed, and highest operational network accessibility. China Railway has solved technical problems such as the construction of Qinghai–Xizang railway and Sichuan–Xizang railway. With the advent of the information age, China's high-speed railway has realized the "dual network integration" of high-speed railway network and the Internet, and launched services such as

electronic ticket, mobile payment, online seat selection, facial recognition, and online food ordering to satisfy people with more travel experiences.

The high-speed railway Huzhou railway station was officially put into use on July 1, 2013, with a total construction area of 19,920 square meters. The main design of the station building is like an egret spreading its wings, symbolizing the economic leap of Huzhou. After the opening of the Huzhou–Hangzhou section of the Hefei–Hangzhou high-speed railway, the development of the Huzhou railway hub has become smoother, and the "Huzhou on the track" has accelerated. The Huzhou–Hangzhou section has become an important connection line of the Zhejiang railway network, which will boost the construction of the inter-city rail network in the Yangtze River Delta and comprehensively build a one hour traffic circle in Zhejiang. The Huzhou–Hangzhou section of the Hefei–Hangzhou high-speed railway spans many areas of Huzhou and Hangzhou. People can enjoy both the scenery of Huzhou and the Fuchun River in Hangzhou by taking this train, which is truly breathtaking.

The rapid construction of high-speed rail has driven the economic development of Huzhou, Zhejiang. Huzhou has been known as the "Silk Palace" since ancient times, both domestically and internationally. From the silk fragments unearthed from Qianshanyang Archaeological Site, it can be seen that Huzhou silk has a history of over 4,700 years and Huzhou is one of the earliest birthplaces for mulberry cultivation, sericulture, and silk weaving to date. In 2015, it was named the "Source of World Silk". In recent years, with the transformation and upgrading of the silk industry, Huzhou has formed a complete industrial chain from planting mulberry and sericulture, silk reeling and weaving, printing, dyeing and finishing, to the export of end products. The "Source of World Silk" has opened a "new Silk Road" riding the wave of China's high-speed rail, selling many high-quality silk products to various parts of the world.

Huzhou also has many delicacies, among which Mogan Bamboo Shoots, Gelao Pickled Chicken, Huzhou Big Wonton, Zhulaoda Zongzi, Xinshi Mutton, Deqing Shrimp, Zhongguan Old Duck Pot, the Taihu Lake Four Delicacies, Leidian Watermelon, the Taihu Lake Goose, etc. are all local specialties. The Huzhou Writing Brush, along with the Huizhou Inkstick, the Xuan Paper and the Duan Inkstone, is known as the "Four Treasures of the Study" and is an important symbol of the centuried and brilliant Chinese civilization.

 **Think and discuss**

1. Make a travel plan for taking high-speed rail and experience the speed and services of China's high-speed rail.

2. Compare the advantages and disadvantages of high-speed rail transportation with other means of transportation.

3. Which countries can China's exported goods be delivered to through railway transportation?

4. What are the specialties of Huzhou, Zhejiang?

5. What other countries also produce silk besides China?

课后练习

一、单选题

1. 下面哪种茶叶产自湖州地区？

A. 龙井茶

B. 安吉白茶

C. 乌龙茶

2. 下列哪个是"文房四宝"之一？

A. 湖笔

B. 筷子

C. 算盘

3. 相传谁发明了毛笔？

A. 孔子

B. 孟子

C. 蒙恬

4. 湖州是哪个文化的发源地？

A. 咖啡文化

B. 酒文化

C. 丝绸文化

5. 世界上第一部茶文化专著是哪本书？

A.《论语》

B.《茶经》

C.《圣经》

6. 谁写了《茶经》这本著作？

A. 陆羽

B. 李白

C. 杜甫

二、判断题

1. 从杭州坐高铁去湖州需要 3 个小时。（　　）

2. 中国高铁先后破解了青藏铁路、川藏铁路建设等技术难题。
（　　）

3. 中国高铁的车次一般以字母 G 开头。（　　）

4. 乘坐中国高铁不可以使用移动支付、在线选座、刷脸进站等功能。
（　　）

After-class exercises

I. Single choice

1. Which tea is originated in Huzhou area?

A. Longjing tea.

B. Anji White tea.

C. Oolong tea.

2. Which of the following is one of the "Four Treasures of the Study"?

A. Writing brush produced in Huzhou.

B. Chopsticks.

C. Abacus.

3. Who invented the Chinese brush according to legend?

A. Confucius.

B. Mencius.

C. Meng Tian.

4. Which culture originated in Huzhou?

A. Coffee culture.

B. Wine culture.

C. Silk culture.

5. What is the world's first book on tea culture?

A. *The Analects of Confucius.*

B. *The Classic of Tea.*

C. Bible.

6. Who wrote *The Classic of Tea*?

A. Lu Yu.

B. Li Bai.

C. Du Fu.

II. True or false

1. It takes three hours to get to Huzhou by high-speed railway from Hangzhou. (   )

2. China high-speed railway has solved technical problems such as

the construction of the Qinghai–Xizang railway and the Sichuan–Xizang railway. (   )

3. The train letter of China high-speed railway generally starts with G. (   )

4. You can't use mobile payment, online seat selection, facial check-in and other functions on China high-speed railway. (   )

（浙江湖州　许飞燕供图）

第三章　教育科技

（杭州孔庙举办纪念孔子诞辰2574周年活动　王晓华供图）

第一课　中国教育

更多讲解，请扫码观看

　　中国有着尊师重教的传统。中国古代的教育体系大体可以分为官学和私学两种形式。官学主要是针对官员进行教育，培养他们的才能和素质。用来选拔官员的科举考试制度建立于隋朝，完善于唐朝。宋朝时期，官学逐渐形成了独特的风貌，成为国家重要的教育形式。私学是中国古代民间教育的一种形式，其起源可追溯到先秦时期，其中，孔子私学规模最大，影响最深。私学主要是由私人或家族创办，为普通民众提供教育服务。书院是唐宋至明清出现的一种独立的教育机构，是私人或官府所设的聚徒讲授、研究学

153

问的场所。著名的四大书院一般是指河南商丘的应天书院、湖南长沙的岳麓书院、江西庐山的白鹿洞书院和河南登封的嵩阳书院。

中华人民共和国成立后，中国政府高度重视教育，制定了一系列教育政策。中国现行的教育制度主要分为学前教育、初等教育、中等教育、高等教育四个阶段。中国的学前教育一般从三岁开始，为三年制。在中国的大部分地区，小学为六年制，但是在一些省份，小学为五年制。小学生通常要学习语文、数学、英语、科学、体育、音乐、美术、信息技术、道德与法治等课程。初中教育一般为三年制，学生在九年级（即初三年级）将面临初级中学升学考试，即中考。依据相关法律，中国目前实施的是九年义务教育的政策。高中教育也是三年制，高中毕业生可参加普通高等学校招生全国统一考试，即高考。

教育是社会发展的基石。党的二十大报告提出，教育、科技、人才是全面建设社会主义现代化国家的基础性、战略性支撑。必须坚持科技是第一生产力、人才是第一资源、创新是第一动力，深入实施科教兴国战略、人才强国战略、创新驱动发展战略，开辟发展新领域新赛道，不断塑造发展新动能新优势。中国政府坚持办好人民满意的教育，完善科技创新体系，加快实施创新驱动发展战略，深入实施人才强国战略。

课堂思考与讨论

1. 比较中国教育的起源和你的国家教育的起源。

2. 在你的国家基础教育阶段学生主要学习哪些课程?

3. 比较中国的大学教育和你的国家的大学教育的异同。

4. 介绍你的大学。

5. 你认为教育最重要的内容是什么?

Education of China

China has a tradition of respecting teachers and valuing education. The education system in ancient China can be roughly divided into two forms: official education and private education. Official education is mainly aimed at educating officials and cultivating their talents and qualities. In early China, educated officials were appointed to manage the country, and the imperial examination system used to select officials was established in the Sui Dynasty and improved in the Tang Dynasty. During the Song Dynasty, official schools gradually formed a unique style and became an important form of education in the country. Private education was a form of folk education in ancient China, with its origins dating back to the pre-Qin period. Confucius' private education had the largest scale and deepest influence. Private schools are mainly founded by individuals or families to provide educational services to the general public. Academies were an independent educational institution that emerged from the Tang and Song to the Ming and Qing dynasties. They were places set up by individuals or officials to gather students to teach and study knowledge. The four famous academies in China are Yingtian Academy in Shangqiu, Henan, Yuelu Academy in Changsha, Hunan, White Deer Grotto Academy in Lushan, Jiangxi, and Songyang Academy in Dengfeng, Henan.

After the founding of the People's Republic of China, the Chinese government attached great importance to education and formulated a series of educational policies and measures. The current education system in China is divided into four stages: preschool education, primary education, secondary education, higher education. Preschool education in China generally starts at the age of three and is a three-year program. In most regions of China, primary school is divided into six years, but in some provinces, primary school is a five-year program. Students usually need to study courses such as Chinese, mathematics, English, science, sports, music, art, information technology, morality and rule of law. Junior high school education is generally a three-year system, and students in 9th grade (3rd grade of junior high school) will take the entrance examination for middle school, that is, Zhongkao. According to relevant laws, China currently implements a policy of nine-year compulsory education, which is free of charge. High school education is also a three-year system, and high school graduates can take part in the Nationwide Unified Examination for Admissions to General Universities and Colleges, namely Gaokao.

Education is the cornerstone of social development. The report of the 20th National Congress of the CPC proposed that education, science and technology, and talents are the basic and strategic support for building a modern socialist country in an all-round way. We must regard science and technology as our primary productive force, talent as our primary resource, and innovation as our primary driver of growth. We will fully implement the strategy for invigorating China through science and education, the workforce development strategy, and the innovation-driven development strategy. We will open up new areas and new arenas in development and steadily foster new growth drivers and new strengths. The Chinese government insists on providing education that satisfies the people, improving the system of scientific and technological innovation, accelerating the implementation of the innovation driven development strategy, and deepening the implementation of the workforce development strategy.

 Think and discuss

1. Compare the origin of education in China with the origin of education in your country.

2. What courses do students mainly study during the basic education stage in your country?

3. Compare the similarities and differences between Chinese university education and your country's university education.

4. Introduce your university.

5. What do you think is the most important content of education?

课后练习

一、判断题

1. 中国古代的教育体系大体可以分为官学和私学两种形式。（   ）

2. 著名的四大书院一般指清华大学、北京大学、浙江大学和复旦大学。（   ）

二、单选题

1. 中国古代用来选拔官员的科举考试制度建立于＿＿＿＿，完善于唐朝。

A. 秦朝　　　　　B. 汉朝　　　　　C. 隋朝

2. 私学是中国古代民间教育的一种形式，其起源可追溯到先秦时期，其中，＿＿＿＿私学规模最大，影响最深。

A. 孔子　　　　　B. 孟子　　　　　C. 庄子

3. ＿＿＿＿是唐宋至明清出现的一种独立的教育机构，是私人或官府所设的聚徒讲授、研究学问的场所。

A. 官学　　　　　B. 书院　　　　　C. 私学

4. 中国的学前教育一般从三岁开始，为＿＿＿＿。

A. 两年制　　　　B. 三年制　　　　C. 四年制

5. 在中国的大部分地区，小学为＿＿＿＿。

A. 五年制　　　　B. 六年制　　　　C. 七年制

6. 中国目前实施的是＿＿＿＿义务教育的政策。

A. 六年　　　　　B. 九年　　　　　C. 十二年

7. 高中毕业生可参加普通高等学校招生全国统一考试，即＿＿＿＿。

A. 面试　　　　　B. 中考　　　　　C. 高考

After-class exercises

I. True or false

1. The education system in ancient China can be roughly divided into two forms: official education and private education. (   )

2. The four famous academies generally refer to Tsinghua University, Peking University, Zhejiang University, and Fudan University. (   )

II. Single choice

1. The imperial examination system used to select officials in ancient China was established in the _____ and improved during the Tang Dynasty.

A. Qin Dynasty   B. Han Dynasty   C. Sui Dynasty

2. Private education is a form of folk education in ancient China, which can be traced back to the pre-Qin period. Among them, _____ private education has the largest scale and the deepest influence.

A. Confucius'   B. Mencius'   C. Zhuangzi's

3. The _____ was an independent educational institution that emerged from the Tang and Song to the Ming and Qing dynasties. It was a place set up by individuals or officials to gather students to teach and study

knowledge.

    A. official school   B. academy   C. private school

    4. Preschool education in China generally starts at the age of three, which is a _____.

    A. two-year system   B. three-year system   C. four-year system

    5. In most parts of China, primary school is a _____.

    A. five-year system   B. six-year system   C. seven-year system

    6. China currently implements a policy of _____ compulsory education.

    A. six-year   B. nine-year   C. twelve-year

    7. High school graduates can participate in the Nationwide Unified Examination for Admissions to General Universities and Colleges, namely _____.

    A. Interview   B. Zhongkao   C. Gaokao

（北京孔庙和国子监博物馆 吴雅云供图）

钱塘新区报
QIANTANG NEW AREA DAILY

2022年3月23日 星期三
责任编辑：何思源 校对：徐韵梅
7 教育

卢旺达小伙的"钱塘学业创业"记

（媒体关于浙江工商大学国际生参加中国"互联网＋"大学生创新创业大赛的报道）

第二课　国际生的网络生活

更多讲解，请扫码观看

网络改变了生活，也走进了教育。网络时代，国际生的学习和生活都发生了重要的变化。

1. 学习：以"互联网＋教育"为例。"互联网＋教育"是指互联网科技与教育相结合的一种新的教育形式。现在，互联网在助力教育公平、增加教育效能、拓展教育路径、提升教育质量等各方面发挥着作用。对国际生来说，互联网已经是完成学习必备的工具之一。以在线学习为例，截至2024年1月底，中国上线慕课数量已超过7万门，选课人次接近13亿，在校学生获得慕课学分人次超过

4亿。近年来，互联网与教育和学习深度融合，中国在线课程的数量和学习人数都保持着快速增长的态势，线上线下混合型课程也得到了深度开发。

2. 购物：以电子商务为例。互联网在中国的发展可以追溯到20世纪80年代末90年代初期。在2000年前后，中国的互联网用户规模逐渐扩大，并形成了一个比较成熟的互联网行业，出现了众多的网站和互联网企业。21世纪10年代初期，移动互联网开始兴起，中国电子商务进入了一个全新的阶段。随着移动支付的出现，电子商务市场的规模不断扩大，越来越多的人开始通过手机进行购物。2015年，中国电子商务市场总交易额突破20万亿元，超过了美国电子商务市场总交易额。中国电子商务市场成为世界上最大的电子商务市场。党的二十大报告指出："加快发展数字经济，促进数字经济和实体经济深度融合。"在这一时代背景下，中国教育部与各地方政府、各高校共同主办了中国"互联网＋"大学生创新创业大赛，旨在深化高等教育综合改革，激发大学生的创造力，培养造就"大众创业、万众创新"的主力军。国际学生在这一比赛中也积极参与，展现出创新创业的能力和魅力。

3. 出行：以共享单车为例。共享单车是一种基于互联网的出行方式，通过手机应用程序进行租借、开锁和支付等操作，用户可以随时随地使用自行车出行。共享单车在中国的发展经历了起步、扩张和调整3个阶段。2016年至2017年，共享单车企业大量涌现，投入巨资进行市场扩张。行业的发展为人们带来了出行的便利，但同时也引发了乱停乱放、车辆损坏和秩序混乱等问题。约至2018年，经历了整顿、转型和减量之后，行业规模得到了合理控制，服务质量也得到了提升。现在，在校园里，

管理规范的共享单车为学生们出行提供了极大的便利，深受中国学生和国际学生的好评。

4. 娱乐：以网络游戏为例。网络游戏是指通过计算机网络进行游戏的一种娱乐形式，随着互联网的快速发展，网络游戏行业也得到了蓬勃发展。中国是全球最大的网络游戏市场之一，拥有超过 5 亿的游戏玩家。网络游戏开发公司也在不断壮大，腾讯、网易、盛大等公司成为网络游戏行业的领军者。玩网络游戏是国际学生比较喜欢的休闲方式。

 课堂思考与讨论

1. 与传统商业模式相比，电子商务有什么优缺点？

2. 谈谈你的国家电子商务的发展现状。

3. 如果你参加中国"互联网＋"大学生创新创业大赛，你准备做什么项目？

4. 人工智能技术的发展将为你所学习的专业带来什么机遇和挑战？

5. 介绍一个你玩过的网络游戏。

Online Life of International Students

The internet has changed people's lives and also influenced the idea and methods of education. In the era of the internet, the learning and life of international students have undergone significant changes.

1. Learning in the Internet Age: Take "Internet plus education" as an example. "Internet plus education" refers to a new form of education combining Internet technology and education. Nowadays, the Internet plays a role in promoting educational equity, increasing educational efficiency, expanding educational paths, and improving educational quality. For international students, the internet has become one of the essential tools for completing their studies. Taking online learning as an example, as of the end of January 2024, the number of online MOOCs (Massive Open Online Courses) in China has exceeded 70,000, with nearly 1,300 million course selections and over 400 million students receiving MOOCs credits. In recent years, the Internet has deeply integrated with education and learning, and the number of online courses and learners has maintained a rapid growth trend. The mixed online and offline courses have also been deeply developed.

2. Shopping in the Internet Age: Take e-commerce as an example. The development of internet in China can be traced back to the late 1980s and early 1990s. Around the year 2000, the scale of internet users in China gradually expanded, forming a relatively mature internet industry, with numerous websites and internet companies emerging. In the early 2010s,

mobile internet began to rise, and China's e-commerce entered a new stage. With the emergence of mobile payments, the scale of the e-commerce market continues to expand, and more and more people are starting to shop through mobile phones. In 2015, the total transaction volume of China's e-commerce market has exceeded 20 trillion yuan, surpassing the total transaction volume of the US e-commerce market. China's e-commerce market has become the world's largest e-commerce market. The report of the 20th National Congress of the Communist Party of China pointed out: "We will accelerate the development of the digital economy, further integrate it with the real economy." In this era, the Ministry of Education of China, together with different levels of governments and universities, co-hosted the "Internet +" Undergraduate Innovation and Entrepreneurship Competition, aiming to deepen the comprehensive reform of higher education, stimulate the creativity of college students, and cultivate the main force of "mass entrepreneurship and innovation". International students also actively participated in and demonstrated their ability and charm in innovation and entrepreneurship in this competition.

3. Transportation in the Internet Age: Take bike-sharing as an example. Bike-sharing is an internet-based travel method that allows users to rent, unlock, and pay through mobile apps, allowing them to use bicycles anytime, anywhere. The development of bike-sharing in China has gone through three stages: initiation, expansion, and adjustment. From 2016 to 2017, a large number of bike-sharing companies emerged, investing heavily

in market expansion, bringing convenient modes of transportation, However, it also caused problems such as disorderly parking, vehicle damage, and market disorder. By around 2018, thanks to the rectification, transformation, and reduction, the industry size had been reasonably controlled, and service quality had also been improved. Nowadays, on campus, standardized shared bicycles provide great convenience for students to travel, and are highly praised by Chinese and international students.

4. Entertainment in the Internet Age: Take online gaming as an example. Online gaming refers to a form of entertainment, that is, playing games through network. With the rapid development of the internet, the online gaming industry has also flourished. China is one of the largest online gaming markets in the world, with over 500 million game players. Online gaming development companies are also constantly growing, with companies such as Tencent, NetEase, and Shanda becoming leaders in the online gaming industry. Playing online games is a favorite leisure way for international students.

 Think and discuss

1. What are the advantages and disadvantages of e-commerce compared to traditional business models?

2. Talk about the current status of e-commerce development in your country.

3. If you participate in the China "Internet +" Undergraduate Innovation and Entrepreneurship Competition, what project will you do?

4. What opportunities and challenges will the development of artificial intelligence technology bring to the major you are studying?

5. Introduce an online game you have enjoyed.

课后练习

一、单选题

1. _____年代初期，移动互联网开始兴起，中国电子商务进入了一个全新的阶段。

A. 2000   B. 2010   C. 2020

2. 随着_____的出现，电子商务市场的规模不断扩大，越来越多的人开始通过手机进行购物。

A. 电脑　　　　B. 网络　　　　C. 移动支付

二、填空题

1. 中国教育部与各地方政府、各高校共同主办了_____，旨在深化高等教育综合改革，激发大学生的创造力，培养造就"大众创业、万众创新"的主力军。

2. _____是一种基于互联网的出行方式，通过手机应用程序进行租借、开锁和支付等操作，用户可以随时随地使用自行车出行。

3. _____是指通过计算机网络进行游戏的一种娱乐形式，随着互联网的快速发展，这一行业也得到了蓬勃发展。

三、判断题

1. 约至 2018 年，经历了整顿、转型和减量之后，共享单车行业规模得到了合理控制，服务质量也得到了提升。（　　　）

2. 最近几年，共享单车在中国蓬勃发展。（　　　）

3. 网络游戏开发公司也在不断壮大，腾讯、网易、盛大等公司成为网络游戏行业的领军者。（　　　）

After-class exercises

I. Single choice

1. In the early _____, mobile internet began to rise, and China's e-commerce entered a new stage.

A. 2000s   B. 2010s   C. 2020s

2. With the emergence of _____, the scale of the e-commerce market continues to expand, and more and more people are starting to shop through mobile phones.

A. computer   B. network   C. mobile payment

II. Filling in the blanks

1. The Chinese Ministry of Education, along with different levels of governments and various universities, jointly organized _____ , aiming to deepen the comprehensive reform of higher education, stimulate the creativity of college students, and cultivate the main force for "mass entrepreneurship and innovation".

2. _____ is an internet-based travel method that allows users to rent, unlock, and pay through mobile apps, allowing them to use bicycles

anytime and anywhere.

3. _____ refers to a form of entertainment in which games are played through network. With the rapid development of the internet, this industry has also flourished.

III. True or false

1. By around 2018, thanks to the rectification, transformation, and reduction, the scale of the bike-sharing industry had been reasonably controlled and the service quality had also been improved. (　　)

2. Shared bicycles have developed a lot in China in recent years. (　　)

3. Online gaming development companies are also constantly growing, with companies such as Tencent, NetEase, and Shanda becoming leaders in the online gaming industry. (　　)

话题四　感知中国经济

- 第一章　对外贸易

- 第二章　电子商务

- 第三章　百年企业

第一章　对外贸易

（丝绸之路上的新疆古城　王晓华供图）

第一课　共建"一带一路"

更多讲解，请扫码观看

"一带一路"是指丝绸之路经济带和21世纪海上丝绸之路，涵盖中国历史上丝绸之路和海上丝绸之路途经的中国大陆、中亚、北亚、西亚、印度洋沿岸、地中海沿岸、南美和大西洋地区。这是中国政府于2013年发起倡议建设并主导的跨国经济带。该倡议旨在发展中国与东南亚、南亚、中东、北非和欧洲国家之间的经济合作。其中，新疆被定位为"丝绸之路经济带核心区"，福建为"21世纪海上丝绸之路核心区"。

为推动共建"一带一路"，建立了丝路

基金、亚洲基础设施投资银行、中巴经济走廊等，同时，还发展了中欧班列、中蒙俄经济走廊，建设了中国—中南半岛经济走廊、孟中印缅经济走廊、中国—中亚—西亚经济走廊等，以推进区域全面经济伙伴关系，积极与各地区进行对接合作。截至2023年，中国已与150多个国家和30多个国际组织签署共建"一带一路"合作文件。

　　共建"一带一路"坚持共商共建共享的原则。这一倡议致力于为共同发展繁荣铺平道路，促进各国在设施、贸易、资金、民心等全方位多领域互联互通。共建"一带一路"加强了共建国家和地区之间的经济联系，提供了商品交易的市场，为各地区带来更多新的就业机会，也促进了技术交流。与此同时，也加深了共建国家之间的政治互信和人文交流，不断深化在教育、体育、旅游等领域的合作。共建"一带一路"不仅为相关国家带来切实的利益，也推动了经济全球化的健康发展，是构建人类命运共同体的重大实践。

 课堂思考与讨论

1. "一带一路"是什么意思？你所在的国家是共建国家吗？

2. 查资料，试着在世界地图上指出共建"一带一路"的线路。

3. 查资料，了解共建"一带一路"给你的国家或者共建国家带来的变化，并在课上交流。

4. *你的国家实施了哪些促进对外经贸发展的战略措施？*

The Belt and Road Initiative

"The Belt and Road" refers to the Silk Road Economic Belt and the 21st Century Maritime Silk Road, covering the Chinese mainland, Central Asia, North Asia, West Asia, the Indian Ocean coast, the Mediterranean coast, South America and the Atlantic Ocean through which China's historic Silk Road and Maritime Silk Road passed. This is a transnational economic belt initiated and led by the Chinese government in 2013. The initiative aims to develop economic cooperation between China and countries in Southeast Asia, South Asia, the Middle East, North Africa and Europe. Among them, Xinjiang is positioned as the "core area of the Silk Road Economic Belt" and Fujian is the "core area of the 21st Century Maritime Silk Road".

To promote the Belt and Road Initiative, the Silk Road Fund, the Asian Infrastructure Investment Bank and the China–Pakistan Economic Corridor have been established. At the same time, the China–Europe Railway Express, the China–Mongolia–Russia Economic Corridor, and built the China–Indochina Peninsula Economic Corridor, the Bangladesh–China–India–Myanmar Economic Corridor, the China–Central Asia–West Asia

Economic Corridor and so on have been developed to advance the Regional Comprehensive Economic Partnership. China will actively coordinate and cooperate with other regions. By 2023, China had signed Belt and Road cooperation documents with more than 150 countries and over 30 international organizations.

The Belt and Road Initiative also adheres to the principle of extensive consultation, joint contribution and shared benefits. This initiative is committed to paving the way for common development and prosperity, promoting all-round connectivity in various fields such as facilities, trade, funds and people's communication. The construction of "The Belt and Road" has strengthened economic ties between countries and regions along the route, provided a market for commodity trading, brought more new job opportunities to various regions, and promoted technological exchanges. At the same time, political mutual trust and people-to-people and cultural exchanges between countries along the Belt and Road have also been deepened, and cooperation in education, sports, tourism and other fields has been strengthened. The Belt and Road Initiative has not only brought tangible benefits to relevant countries, but also promoted the sound development of economic globalization. It is a major practice in building a community with a shared future for mankind.

Think and discuss

1. What does "The Belt and Road" mean? Is your country a participant along the route?

2. Check the information and try to point out the route of "The Belt and Road" on the world map.

3. Check materials to understand the changes brought about by the construction of "The Belt and Road" to your country or countries along the route and exchange opinions in class.

4. What strategic measures has your country implemented to promote foreign economic and trade development?

课后练习

一、判断题

1. 共建"一带一路"不仅加强了各国经济联系,也促进了技术交流。
(　　)

2. 共建"一带一路"只注重经济合作,对文化、教育、体育方面的交流不产生影响。(　　)

3. 中欧班列是共建"一带一路"项目之一。(　　)

二、单选题

1. "一带一路"倡议发起于_____年。

A.2003　　　　　B.2013　　　　C.2020

2. 目前,中国已经与_____多个国家和_____多个国际组织建立共建"一带一路"合作关系。

A.140；30　　　B.150；30　　C.120；20

3. 共建"一带一路"坚持_____的原则。

A. 合作共赢　　B. 自由贸易　　C. 共商共建共享

4. ＿＿＿＿是"丝绸之路经济带核心区"。

A. 新疆　　　　B. 西安　　　　C. 杭州

After-class exercises

I. True of false

1. The Belt and Road Initiative not only strengthens economic ties among countries, but also promotes technological exchanges. (　　)

2. The Belt and Road Initiative only focuses on economic cooperation and has no impact on exchanges in culture, education and sports. (　　)

3. The China–Europe Railway Express is one of the Belt and Road projects. (　　)

II. Single choice

1. The Belt and Road Initiative was launched in ＿＿＿＿.

A. 2003　　　　B. 2013　　C. 2020

2. At present, China has established Belt and Road cooperation relations

with more than _____ countries and over _____ international organizations.

    A.140; 30   B.150; 30   C.120; 20

3. The Belt and Road Initiative adheres to the principle of _____.

A. win-win cooperation

B. free trade

C. extensive consultation, joint contribution and shared benefits

4. _____ is the "core area of the Silk Road Economic Belt".

    A. Xinjiang   B. Xi'an   C. Hangzhou

（浙江桐庐　徐蓓佳供图）

第二课　快递之乡

更多讲解，请扫码观看

随着中国经济，特别是互联网经济的迅猛发展，物流行业也得到了快速的进步。从最初的"以物易物"到现在物流网络覆盖全国，中国的物流行业已经成为世界上最具活力和竞争力的行业之一，成为经济发展的重要支柱。近年来，物流行业规模不断扩大，技术力量不断提升。未来，物流行业也将继续走智能化、绿色环保和全球化的道路，迎接新的发展阶段。从 2013 年至 2023 年，中国快递单量连年增长，从不足 100 亿件到突破 1000 亿件，稳居世界第一；这 10 年，中国跑出 300 万名"快递小哥"，支撑起全世界最庞大复杂的物流系统，这背后投射的是中国实体经济和数字经济的高速发展。随着快递业的迅猛发展，中国目前已经拥有顺丰、申通、中通、圆通、韵达、宅急送、中国邮政、京东、德邦、百世等主流快递公司。

物流行业的高速发展，也带动了浙江经济的发展。杭州市的桐庐县，地处于浙江省西北部地区，它的面积不大，只有 1829 平方公里，人口也不多，截至 2023 年，只有 46 万人，但是 2023 年桐庐县地区生产总值 469 亿元，对于一个小县城而言，是一个相当不错的水平。30 多年前，一批桐庐人在改革开放的浪潮中奋勇前行，在全国各地创办快递企业，其中就包括申通、中通、圆通、韵达 4 家著名的快递公司，占据中国快递行业的"半壁江山"，它们的总部都位于桐庐，因此，桐庐被誉为"快递之乡"。近些年来，桐庐积极寻求转型，大力推动快递物流产业的发展，成功地从传统的"单一产业链"转向了现代化的"综合生态圈"。此外，桐庐也在努力实现由"快递人之乡"向"快递物流产业之乡"的转变，进一步提升其作为"中国民营快递之乡"的知名度。

 课堂思考与讨论

1. 介绍一下你家乡的快递物流公司。

2. 目前中国快递物流业还有什么不足之处？

3. 你认为桐庐能成为快递之乡的关键因素是什么?

4. 中国快递业的未来将如何发展?

Hometown of Express Delivery

With the rapid development of the Chinese economy, especially the internet economy, the logistics industry has also made rapid progress. From the initial "Barter" to the present logistics network covering the whole country, China's logistics industry has become one of the most dynamic and competitive industries in the world and an important pillar of economic development. In recent years, the scale of the industry has been continuously expanding, and the technological strength has been continuously improving. In the future, it will continue to take the path of intelligence, green environmental protection, and globalization to welcome a new stage of development. From 2013 to 2023, China's express delivery volume has grown year by year, from less than 10 billion units to over 100 billion units, firmly ranking first in the world. Over the past decade, China has produced three million "express delivery guys" out of nowhere, supporting the world's largest and most complex logistics system, reflecting the rapid development of China's real and digital economy. With the rapid development of the express industry, China now has such mainstream express companies as SF Express, STO Express, ZTO Express, YTO

Express, Yunda Express, ZJS Express, China Post, JDL Express, Deppon Express, and Best.

The rapid development of the logistics industry has also driven the economic development of Zhejiang. Tonglu County in Hangzhou is located in the northwest of the province. It has a small area of only 1,829 square kilometers and a small population of only about 460,000 people by 2023. But in 2023, Tonglu County's gross domestic product reached 46.9 billion yuan, which was a pretty good level for a small county. More than 30 years ago, a group of Tonglu people bravely advanced in the wave of reform and opening up, establishing express delivery enterprises in various parts of the country, including four express delivery companies, STO Express, ZTO Express, YTO Express, and Yunda Express, which occupy half of China's express delivery industry. Their headquarters are located in Tonglu, so Tonglu has become a truly "hometown of express delivery". In recent years, Tonglu has taken the initiative to seek change and vigorously developed the express logistics industry, achieving a transformation from a "single industrial chain" to a "comprehensive ecosystem", accelerating the transformation from a "hometown of express delivery people" to a "hometown of express logistics industry", and continuously polishing the brand of "hometown of private express delivery in China".

Think and discuss

1. Introduce the express logistics company in your hometown.

2. What are the shortcomings of China's express logistics industry at present?

3. What are the key factors that make Tonglu the hometown of express delivery?

4. How will China's express delivery industry develop in the future?

课后练习

一、填空题

1. 2013 年至 2023 年，中国快递单量从不足_____件到突破

_____件。

2. 中国经济发展的重要支柱是_____。

3. 随着_____，特别是_____的快速发展，物流行业也得到了迅猛的进步。

4. 截至 2023 年，桐庐县有_____万人口。

5. 近年来，桐庐主动求变，大力发展快递物流产业，实现了从_____向_____的转变。

二、单选题

1. 桐庐的别称是什么？

A. 快递之城

B. 快递之乡

C. 物流王国

D. 快递天堂

2. 下面哪个快递公司不是在桐庐注册创立的？

A. 顺丰

B. 申通

C. 中通

D. 韵达

3. 桐庐位于浙江省哪个地区？

A. 东部

B. 南部

C. 西北部

D. 东南部

4.2023 年桐庐县地区生产总值超过了多少亿元？

A.300 亿元

B.200 亿元

C.500 亿元

D.400 亿元

三、多选题

目前，中国有哪些主流快递公司？

A. 顺丰

B. 韵达

C. 申通

D. 中通

After-class exercises

I. Filling in the blanks

1. From 2013 to 2023, China's express delivery volume has grown from

less than _____ pieces to over _____ pieces.

2. An important pillar of China's economic development is _____ .

3. With the rapid development of the _____ , especially the _____ , the logistics industry has also made rapid progress.

4. By 2023, the population of Tonglu County is _____ .

5. In recent years, Tonglu has taken the initiative to seek change and vigorously developed the express logistics industry, achieving a transformation from a _____ to a _____ .

II. Single choice

1. What is the alternative name of Tonglu?

A. The city of express delivery.

B. The hometown of express delivery.

C. The kingdom of logistics.

D. The paradise of express delivery.

2. Which courier company below was not registered and established in Tonglu?

A. SF Express.

B. STO Express.

C. ZTO Express.

D. Yunda Express.

3. Which region is Tonglu located in Zhejiang Province?

A. The east.

B. The south.

C. The northwest.

D. The southeast.

4. How many billion yuan did the gross domestic product of Tonglu County exceed in 2023?

A. 30 billion yuan.

B. 20 billion yuan.

C. 50 billion yuan.

D. 40 billion yuan.

III. Multiple choice

Currently, what are the mainstream express delivery companies in China?

A. SF Express.

B. Yunda Express.

C. STO Express.

D. ZTO Express.

第二章　电子商务

（中国义乌小商品城　叶卫挺供图）

第一课　跨境电商

更多讲解，请扫码观看

跨境电商已经成为浙江省的一项重要产业，越来越多的企业开始涉足跨境电商领域。统计数据显示，浙江省跨境电商交易额已经连续多年保持增长。2019年，浙江省跨境电商交易额达到了1.8万亿元，2022年浙江省跨境电商零售进口单量居全国第一。其中，杭州、宁波、温州、义乌等地区成为浙江省跨境电商的主要发展区域。随着全球化的不断推进，跨境电商将会有更大的发展空间，2023年新增跨境电商出口网店1万家以上。未来，随着跨境电商平台的崛起，平台化的竞争将会更加激烈；跨境电商服务将会不断升级，更加智能化、精细化，满足消费者的

个性化需求；跨境电商平台将与物流公司紧密合作，推出更加便捷、快速的物流服务，改善用户体验。

中国义乌小商品城创建于 1982 年，是中国最大的小商品出口基地之一，目前商品已出口到 200 多个国家和地区；同时，义乌小商品市场吸引了来自 80 多个国家的进口商品馆入驻，标志着"买全球货、卖全球货"的商业模式已经初见成效。作为义乌市场创新发展的探索者和实践者，义乌小商品城聚焦数字化转型，抢抓自贸试验区建设等新机遇，于 2020 年 10 月上线"义乌小商品城"官方网站，全面开启了数字化转型发展的新征程。义乌跨境电商借助当地传统小商品的供应链优势，主营品类以小商品为特色，并辐射其他的相关品类。与此同时，义乌良好的经济发展以及营商环境等因素也吸引了大量的跨境电商创业者及从业者，并通过产业园区或特定区域等形成了良好的产业集聚效应；同时随着跨境电商的热潮持续蔓延，越来越多的年轻人，尤其是刚毕业的大学生都纷纷加入跨境电商行业，去实现自己的抱负与梦想。

 课堂思考与讨论

1. 跨境电商在未来应如何发展与转型？

2. 著名的跨境电商企业有哪些？

3. 你家乡有跨境电商企业吗？进行一次考察与访问。

4. 中国义乌小商品城可以快速崛起与发展的秘诀你觉得有哪些？

5. 如果毕业后你也想加入跨境电商行业，你会选择哪类产品进行销售，并如何将其销往全球？

Cross-Border E-Commerce

Cross-border e-commerce has become an important industry in Zhejiang Province, and more and more enterprises are entering the field of cross-border e-commerce. According to statistical data, the cross-border e-commerce transaction volume in Zhejiang Province has maintained growth for many consecutive years. In 2019, the cross-border e-commerce transaction volume in Zhejiang Province reached 1.8 trillion yuan, and in 2022, the retail import volume of cross-border e-commerce in Zhejiang Province ranked first in the country. Among them, Hangzhou, Ningbo, Wenzhou, Yiwu and other regions have become the main development areas for cross-border e-commerce in Zhejiang Province. With the continuous advancement of globalization, cross-border e-commerce will have greater development space, with over 10,000 new cross-border e-commerce export online stores added in 2023. In the future, with the increasing rise of cross-border e-commerce platforms, the competition for platformization will become more intense; cross-border e-commerce services will continue to upgrade, becoming more intelligent and refined to meet the personalized needs of consumers; cross-border e-commerce platforms will work closely with logistics companies to provide more convenient and fast logistics services, so as to improve user experience.

Yiwu China Commodities City, founded in 1982, is one of the largest small commodity export bases in China, with products exported to more than 200 countries and regions at present. At the same time, more than 80 countries and regions have established import commodity pavilions in the Yiwu China Commodities City, and the pattern of "buy from the world; sell to the world" has initially taken shape. As an explorer and practitioner of innovation and development of Yiwu market, Yiwu China Commodities City focused on digital transformation, grabbed new opportunities such as the construction of free trade pilot zone, and launched the official website "Chinagoods.com" in October 2020, comprehensively opening a new journey of digital transformation development. Yiwu cross-border e-commerce leverages the supply chain advantages of local traditional small commodities, with its main category featuring small commodities and radiating to other related categories. At the same time, the favorable economic development and business environment of Yiwu have also attracted a large number of cross-border e-commerce entrepreneurs and practitioners, and have formed a good industrial agglomeration effect through industrial parks or specific regions. Meanwhile, as the trend of cross-border e-commerce continues to spread, more and more young people, especially newly graduated college students, are joining the cross-border e-commerce industry to realize their aspirations and dreams.

 Think and discuss

1.How should cross-border e-commerce develop and transform in the future?

2. What are the famous cross-border e-commerce enterprises?

3. Are there any cross-border e-commerce enterprises in your hometown? Conduct an investigation and visit.

4. What do you think are the secrets of the rapid rise and development of Yiwu China Commodities City?

5. If you also want to join the cross-border e-commerce industry after graduation, which kind of product would you choose to sell and how would you sell it globally?

课后练习

一、判断题

1. 2022 年浙江省跨境电商零售进口单量居全国第一。（　　）

2. 中国义乌小商品城，是中国最大的小商品出口基地之一，创建于 2002 年。（　　）

3. 跨境电商平台将与物流公司紧密合作，推出更加便捷、快速的物流服务，改善用户体验。（　　）

二、单选题

1. 以下哪个地区不是浙江省跨境电商的主要发展区域？

A. 杭州

B. 宁波

C. 温州

D. 南昌

2. 义乌小商品城聚焦数字化转型，抢抓自贸试验区建设等新机遇，于 2020 年 10 月上线"义乌小商品城"官方网站，全面开启了哪种转型模式？

A. 本地化转型模式

B. 数字化转型模式

C. 高端化转型模式

D. 绿色化转型模式

3. 义乌跨境电商借助当地传统小商品的供应链优势，主营品类以什么为特色，并辐射其他的相关品类？

A. 大宗贸易

B. 重工业

C. 小商品

D. 汽车

4. 根据交互模式，以下哪个模式不是跨境电商的主要模式？

A. 计划模式

B. B2B

C. B2C

D. C2C

5. 中国的跨境电商发展特别突出，是什么原因？

A. 科技进步

B. 消费升级

C. 产业基础

D. 以上都是

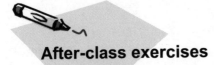

After-class exercises

I. True or false

1. In 2022, the retail import volume of cross-border e-commerce in Zhejiang Province ranked first in the country. (   )

2. Yiwu China Commodities City, founded in 2002, is one of the largest small commodity export bases in China. (   )

3. Cross-border e-commerce platforms will work closely with logistics companies to provide more convenient and fast logistics services, so as to improve user experience. (   )

II. Single choice

1. Which region is not the main development area for cross-border e-commerce in Zhejiang Province?

A. Hangzhou.

B. Ningbo.

C. Wenzhou.

D. Nanchang.

2. Yiwu China Commodities City focused on digital transformation, grabbed new opportunities such as the construction of free trade pilot zone, and launched the official website "Chinagoods.com" in October 2020. Which kind of transformation did Yiwu China Commodities City focus on?

A. Localization transformation.

B. Digital transformation.

C. High-end orientation transformation.

D. Greenization transformation.

3. What are the main product categories of Yiwu cross-border e-commerce, leveraging the supply chain advantages of local traditional small commodities, and radiating to other related categories?

A. Bulk trade.

B. Heavy industry.

C. Small commodities.

D. Vehicles.

4. According to the type of interaction, which mode is not the main modes of cross-border e-commerce?

A. Planning mode.

B. B2B.

C. B2C.

D. C2C.

5. China's cross-border e-commerce development is particularly

prominent, what is (are) the reason(s)?

    A. Technological progress.

    B. Consumption upgrade.

    C. Industry foundation.

    D. Above all.

（支付宝总部　叶卫挺供图）

第二课　阿里巴巴

更多讲解，请扫码观看

马云 1988 年毕业于杭州师范大学，1995年初执教于杭州电子工业学院（现杭州电子科技大学），讲授英文以及国际贸易。1999 年，马云发现互联网可以为中国提供新型商业模式，于是创办了阿里巴巴公司，最初公司只有 18 名员工，办公室非常简陋，没有任何装修和家具。此外，马云还曾多次遭遇资金短缺，公司几乎面临破产。随着时间的推移，马云和他的团队克服了利润不足、技术落后等问

题，强化了公司的竞争力，并开启了全球化的道路。在马云的领导下，阿里巴巴从谷底走向巅峰，成为一个全方位的电子商务企业，最终成为全球知名的电商平台。

2000年，马云在美国亚洲商业协会的年度评选中荣膺"商业领袖"称号，他的名字也出现在《福布斯》杂志的封面上，他还组织了首届"西湖论剑"活动。2000年，阿里巴巴推出供应商服务，并于2002年率先推出"诚信通"业务。2003年，他们创建了名为"淘宝网"的个人电子购物网站，同年还设立了一个第三方支付平台——支付宝。2004年底，马云被中央电视台评选为"中国经济年度人物"。2005年，阿里巴巴成功收购了雅虎中国，马云也被选入2005年十大并购人物之列，而阿里巴巴则成为最佳雇主公司。2006年，阿里巴巴注资口碑网，发展迅速，这使得马云和阿里巴巴获得了包括自主创新优秀成果奖在内的3个重要奖项，阿里巴巴再次被《福布斯》杂志评选为年度"全球最佳B2B网站"。2007年，阿里巴巴创立了阿里软件和阿里妈妈，并吸引了来自中国工商银行的8家基础投资者。同年11月，阿里巴巴在香港再次上市。同年，马云在美国《微电脑世界》杂志评选的全球50大最重要互联网人物中名列前20，马云在IT业以50亿元身价的估值在"2007年胡润IT富豪榜"上位列第8。

短短几年，马云由一个平凡的大学教师成长为世界一流的商业精英，阿里巴巴则由一个小网站发展为世界B2B和C2C市场的领军者，这不得不说是一个奇迹。

课堂思考与讨论

1.在学习、工作与生活中，你是否用到了与阿里巴巴相关的产品与服务？

2.找机会去阿里巴巴参观访问，了解一下阿里巴巴的发展历史。

3.阿里巴巴成功的原因有哪些？

4.介绍一下你所了解的其他电商平台。

5.你认为电子商务和传统商业相比，有什么优势和劣势？

Alibaba

Ma Yun (Jack Ma) graduated from Hangzhou Normal University in 1988 and taught at Hangzhou Institute of Electronic Technology (now Hangzhou Dianzi University) in early 1995, teaching English and international trade. In 1999, Jack Ma discovered that the internet could provide a new business model for China, so he founded Alibaba Group. Initially, the company had only 18 employees and the office was very simple without any decoration or furniture. In addition, Jack Ma has also experienced multiple instances of funding shortages, and the company was almost facing bankruptcy. Over time, Jack Ma and his team overcame problems such as insufficient profits and outdated technology, strengthened the company's competitiveness, and embarked on a path of globalization. Under the leadership of Jack Ma, Alibaba has gone from bottom to top, becoming a comprehensive e-commerce enterprise, and finally becoming a globally renowned e-commerce platform.

In 2000, Jack Ma was selected as the business leader of the year by the Asian Business Association in the United States. Jack Ma appeared on the cover of *Forbes* magazine and organized the first West Lake Cybersecurity Conference. In 2000, Alibaba launched supplier services and took the lead in launching the TrustPass business in 2002. In 2003, Alibaba launched Taobao, a personal electronic shopping website, and established Alipay, a third-party payment platform. At the end of 2004, Ma Yun was rated as China Economic Person of the Year by CCTV. In 2005, Alibaba acquired Yahoo, and Jack Ma was named one of the top 10 M&A figures in 2005, while Alibaba became the best employer company. In 2006, Alibaba invested in Koubei and developed rapidly, madding Jack Ma and Alibaba won three important awards, including the Outstanding Achievement Award for Independent Innovation, and Alibaba was once again selected as the World's Best B2B Website of the Year by *Forbes* magazine. In 2007, Alibaba established Alibaba Software and Alimama, and attracted eight basic investments from Industrial and Commercial Bank of China, and successfully listed again in Hong Kong in November. In the same year, Jack Ma ranked the 20th among the top 50 most important internet figures in the world selected by *PC World* magazine in the United States, and ranked 8th on the 2007 Hurun IT Rich List with a valuation of five billion yuan in the IT industry.

In just a few years, Jack Ma has transformed from an ordinary university teacher to a world-class business elite, while Alibaba has developed from a small website to a leader in the world's B2B and C2C markets, which has to be said to be a miracle.

Think and discuss

1. Have you used Alibaba related products and services in your studies, work, and life?

2. Find opportunities to visit Alibaba and learn about its development history.

3. What are the reasons for Alibaba's success?

4. Introduce other e-commerce platforms that you are familiar with.

5. What advantages and disadvantages do you think e-commerce has compared with traditional commerce?

课后练习

一、判断题

1. 在创立阿里巴巴之前，马云曾经是一名教师，执教于杭州电子工业学院（现杭州电子科技大学）。（　　　）

2. 2009 年，马云发现互联网可以为中国提供新型商业模式，于是创办了阿里巴巴。（　　　）

3. 阿里巴巴是一个全方位的电子商务企业，是全球知名的电商平台。（　　　）

4. 2003 年，阿里巴巴推出个人电子购物网站淘宝网，并成立第三方支付平台——微信支付。（　　　）

5. 马云创业过程中曾多次遭遇资金短缺的情况，公司几乎面临破产。（　　　）

二、单选题

1. 阿里巴巴不仅经营着 B2B 国际贸易，还涉及网上零售、支付平台和云服务等，以下哪个品牌或平台不是阿里巴巴旗下的？

A. 支付宝

B. 淘宝

C. 抖音

D. 阿里云

2. 阿里巴巴在国内面临着很多的竞争对手，不包括以下哪个公司？

A. 拼多多

B. 京东

C. 腾讯

D. 中石化

3. 以下哪个是阿里巴巴的创新模式，也是它获得成功的重要原因之一？

A. 向卖家收取会员费，不向买家收取费用

B. 向买家收取会员费，不向卖家收取费用

C. 不收费用

D. 赚取佣金

4. 阿里云未来将会成为阿里巴巴重要的收入与利润来源。它和我们看到的哪些国际巨头一样？

A. 亚马逊

B. 谷歌

C. 微软

D. 以上都是

5. 以下哪个物流公司属于阿里巴巴，并在其中占据越来越重要的地位？

A. 京东快递

B. 菜鸟

C. 顺丰

D. 中国邮政

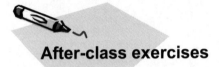

After-class exercises

I. True or false

1. Before founding Alibaba, Jack Ma was a teacher at Hangzhou Institute of Electronic Technology (now Hangzhou Dianzi University). (　　)

2. Jack Ma founded Alibaba in 2009 after discovering that the internet could provide a new business model for China. (　　)

3. Alibaba is a comprehensive e-commerce enterprise and a world-renowned e-commerce platform. (　　)

4. In 2003, Alibaba launched its personal electronic shopping site Taobao and established a third-party payment platform, Wechat Pay. (　　)

5. In the process of entrepreneurship, Jack Ma also encountered a shortage of funds several times, and the company almost faced bankruptcy. (　　)

II. Single choice

1. Alibaba not only operates B2B international trade, but also involves online retail, payment platforms and cloud services, etc. Which of the following brands or platforms is not owned by Alibaba?

A. Alipay.

B. Taobao.

C. Tik Tok.

D. Alibaba Cloud.

2. Alibaba faces a lot of domestic competitors, which of the following companies is not included?

A. Pinduoduo.

B. JD.

C. Tencent.

D. Sinopec.

3. Which of the following is Alibaba's innovation model and one of the important reasons for its success?

A. Charge a membership fee to the seller and no fee to the buyer.

B. Charge a membership fee to the buyer and no fee to the seller.

C. Free of charge.

D. Earn commission.

4. Alibaba Cloud will become an important source of revenue and profit for Alibaba in the future. Which international giant(s) we have seen is

(are) just like it?

    A. Amazon.

    B. Google.

    C. Microsoft.

    D. Above all.

    5. Which of the following logistics companies belongs to Alibaba and occupies an increasingly important position among them?

    A. JDL Express.

    B. Cainiao.

    C. SF Express.

    D. China Post.

（钉钉总部　叶卫挺供图）

第三章 百年企业

天下浙商的精神家园 全球浙商的文化宝库

（杭州浙商博物馆 吴雅云供图）

第一课 儒商浙商

更多讲解，请扫码观看

儒商是指有德行与文化素养的商人，是"儒"（儒家文化）和"商"（商业实践）相结合的一种文化现象。儒商主张以诚信、道德、责任、和谐等传统儒家价值观为商业经营准则，认为商业行为应该符合社会伦理和道德标准，注重企业的社会责任和长远发展。儒商在中国商业文化历史上占有重要地位，代表了中国传统文化和商业文化的结合。儒商对社会发展有忧患意识和崇高责任感，有救世济民的远大抱负，追求"达则兼善天下"。邵逸夫、霍英东等都是儒商的代表。

浙商是指来自中国浙江省或与浙江有密切联系的商人和企业家。浙江素有"商业大省"之称，历史上就有着繁荣的商业贸易，浙商文化有其独特性。浙商与粤商、徽商、晋商，在历史上被合称为"四大商帮"。浙江商人善于创新，勇于拼搏，具有强烈的市场竞争意识和创业精神。他们在中国改革开放后的市场经济中崭露头角，在中国经济史上发挥了重要的作用。

历史上有许多名震中国的浙商。比如，元末明初的"天下首富"湖州人沈万三，清末"中国近代五金行业先驱"叶澄衷（镇海人）。当代浙江也诞生了许多优秀的企业家。根据"胡润百富榜"，在过去的20多年时间里，浙商曾多次问鼎"中国首富"，他们分别是：宗庆后（娃哈哈集团创始人）、马云（阿里巴巴集团主要创始人）、钟睒睒（农夫山泉股份有限公司董事长）、丁磊（网易公司创始人）、陈天桥（盛大网络董事会主席和首席执行官）。其中，马云和钟睒睒一度成为"亚洲首富"。

"敢为天下先、勇于闯天下"，充满创新创业活力的浙商群体为推动浙江经济持续稳定快速发展，为促进中国区域经济协调发展和提升开放型经济水平做出了重要贡献。

 课堂思考与讨论

1. 什么是儒商？

2. 介绍一位浙商。

3. 阿里巴巴集团有 6 个核心价值观：客户第一、团队合作、拥抱变化、诚信、激情、敬业。谈一谈你对这个企业价值观的理解。

4. 你接触过浙江商人吗？谈一谈他们给你留下的印象。

5. 参观浙商博物馆。

Confucian Businessmen and Zhejiang Merchants

Confucian businessmen refer to merchants with moral character and cultural literacy, and are a cultural phenomenon that combines "Confucianism"(Confucian culture) and "business"(commercial practice). Confucian businessmen advocate traditional Confucian values such as integrity, morality, responsibility, and harmony as business management principles, emphasizing that business behaviors should comply with social ethics and moral standards, and emphasizing the social responsibility and long-term development of enterprises. Confucian businessmen hold an important position in the history of Chinese commercial culture, representing the combination of traditional Chinese culture and commercial culture. They have an awareness of potencial dangers, a noble sense of responsibility for social development, and a lofty ambition to save the world and the people. They pursue the goal of achieving excellence while also benefiting the world. Run Run Shaw and Henry Fok are representatives of Confucian businessmen.

Zhejiang merchants refer to merchants and entrepreneurs from Zhejiang Province, or closely related to Zhejiang. Zhejiang is known as the "major commercial province" and has had a prosperous commercial trade in history, so the culture of Zhejiang merchants is also unique and profound. Zhejiang merchants, Guangdong merchants, Huizhou merchants, and Shanxi merchants, have been collectively referred to as the "Four Great Business Groups" in history. Zhejiang merchants are good at innovation, brave in fighting, and have a strong sense of market competition and entrepreneurial spirit. They have emerged and played an important role in the market economy after China's reform and opening up.

In history, there were many famous Zhejiang merchants throughout the country. For example, Shen Wansan, a Huzhou native, was dubbed "the richest man in the world" at the end of the Yuan Dynasty and the beginning of the Ming Dynasty, and Ye Chengzhong, a Zhenhai native at the end of the Qing Dynasty, also a pioneer in China's modern hardware industry. Many outstanding entrepreneurs have also emerged in contemporary Zhejiang. According to the Hurun China Rich List, Zhejiang businessmen have won the title of "China's richest man" for many times in the past 20 years. For example, Zong Qinghou, the founder of Hangzhou Wahaha Group, Ma Yun, the main founder of Alibaba Group, Zhong Shanshan, the chairman of Nongfu Spring, Ding Lei, the founder of NetEase, and Chen Tianqiao, the chairman and CEO of Shanda Network, etc. Among them, Ma Yun and Zhong Shanshan once became the "richest man in Asia".

The group of Zhejiang businessmen who dare to lead the world, have the courage to explore the world, and are full of innovation and entrepreneurship vitality, have made important contributions to promoting the sustained and rapid development of Zhejiang's economy, promoting the coordinated development of China's regional economy, and improving the level of an open economy.

 Think and discuss

1. What is a Confucian businessman?

2. Introduce a Zhejiang businessman.

3. Alibaba Group has six core values: customer first, teamwork, embracing change, integrity, passion, and dedication. Talk about your understanding of the values of this company.

4. Have you had any contact with Zhejiang businessmen? Talk about the impression they left on you.

5. Visit the Zhejiang Merchants Museum.

课后练习

一、填空题

1.＿＿＿＿＿＿是指有德行与文化素养的商人，是"儒"（儒家文化）和"商"（商业实践）相结合的一种文化现象。

2.＿＿＿＿＿＿是指来自中国浙江省或与浙江有密切联系的商人和企业家。

3. 元末明初的"天下首富"湖州人＿＿＿＿＿＿是历史上的著名浙商。

二、单选题

当代中国有许多有名的浙江商人，请问下面哪一位不是浙江商人？

A. 马云　　　　　B. 马化腾　　　　　C. 钟睒睒

三、多选题

1. 儒商主张以＿＿＿＿、和谐等传统儒家价值观为商业经营准则，认为商业行为应该符合社会伦理和道德标准，注重企业的社会责任和长远发展。

　　A. 诚信　　　　　　　　B. 道德　　　　　　　　C. 责任

　　2. 儒商在中国商业文化历史上占有重要地位，代表了中国＿＿＿和＿＿＿的结合。

　　A. 传统文化　　　　　　B. 商业文化　　　　　　C. 道家文化

　　3. 浙江商人＿＿＿＿，具有强烈的市场竞争意识和创业精神。他们在中国改革开放后的市场经济中崭露头角，在中国经济史上发挥了重要的作用。

　　A. 善于创新　　　　　　B. 安于现状　　　　　　C. 勇于拼搏

四、判断题

　　1. 儒商对社会发展有忧患意识和崇高责任感，有救世济民的远大抱负，追求"达则兼善天下"。邵逸夫、霍英东等都是儒商的代表。（　　　）

　　2. "敢为天下先、勇于闯天下"，充满创新创业活力的浙商群体为推动浙江经济持续稳定快速发展，为促进中国区域经济协调发展和提升开放型经济水平做出了重要贡献。（　　　）

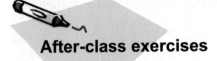

After-class exercises

I. Filling in the blanks

1. _____ refer to merchants with moral character and cultural literacy, which is a cultural phenomenon that combines "Confucianism" (Confucian culture) and "business" (commercial practice).

2. _____ refer to businessmen and entrepreneurs from or closely related to Zhejiang Province, China.

3. _____ , "the richest man in the world" from Huzhou during the late Yuan and the early Ming dynasties, was a famous Zhejiang merchant in history.

II. Single choice

There are many famous Zhejiang merchants in contenporary China. Which of the following is NOT a Zhejiang merchant?

A. Ma Yun.   B. Ma Huateng.   C. Zhong Shanshan.

III. Multiple choices

1. Confucian merchants advocate traditional Confucian values such as _____, and harmony as business principles, believing that business behaviors should comply with social ethics and moral standards, and emphasizing the social responsibility and long-term development of enterprises.

    A. integrity   B. ethics   C. responsibility

2. Confucian merchants hold an important position in the history of Chinese commercial culture, representing the combination of _____ and _____ in China.

    A. traditional culture   B. commercial culture   C. Taoist culture

3. Zhejiang businessmen are _____, and have a strong sense of market competition and entrepreneurial spirit. They have emerged in the market economy after China's reform and opening up, and have played an important role in the history of the Chinese economy.

    A. good at innovation

    B. content with the current situation

    C. brave in fighting

IV. True or false

1. Confucian merchants have an awareness of potential dangers, a sense of concern and lofty responsibility for social development, and have

lofty aspirations to save the world and benefit the people, and pursue the principle of "achieving excellence which also benefiting the world". Run Run Shaw and Henry Fok are representatives of Confucian merchants. (   )

2. The community of Zhejiang merchants, full of innovation and entrepreneurship vitality, has provided guarantees for the sustained, stable and rapid development of Zhejiang's economy, and has made important contributions to promoting coordinated development of China's regional economy and improving the level of an open economy. (   )

（胡庆余堂内景　王晓慧供图）

第二课　胡庆余堂

更多讲解，请扫码观看

　　杭州的胡庆余堂是一家历史悠久的中药企业，被誉为"江南药王"，是中国现存的老字号中药企业之一，由清末商人胡雪岩于1874年创办。1878年，胡庆余堂雪记国药号店堂于杭州大井巷正式开业，下设综合部、制丸粗料部、切片部、原药储存库等10个部门。后来，店堂迁至钱塘江畔。经营多年后，胡庆余堂于1999年改制为胡庆余堂药业有限公司，成为高新技术企业。

　　胡庆余堂最初的药方来自南宋官办药局的局方、传统方剂、名医的验方和秘方等，主要产品包括丸、散、膏、丹等不同的剂型。在由传统向现代发展的过程中，胡庆余堂充分发挥中医药的优势，结合现代科学技术，借鉴现代医药和天然药学的发展经验，不断开发中药、中成药、保健食品的新产品。如今，胡庆余堂已从一家传统医药企业，逐步发展成为集中药材种植、饮片加工、药酒生产、成药制造、连锁药店、医学研究、药膳保健、中医门诊、养生旅游等于一体的产业格局。1996 年，胡庆余堂被授予"中华老字号"证书，2002 年，被认定为中国驰名商标，2006 年，胡庆余堂中药文化被列入第一批国家级非物质文化遗产名录。

胡庆余堂的成立宗旨是济世宁人，意为造福天下人民。百年来，胡庆余堂秉承"采办务真，修制务精"的制药祖训，以及"是乃仁术，真不二价"的经营理念，传承了"戒欺"的诚信经营精神，其品牌和文化精神深深根植于民众心中。胡庆余堂的建筑具有江南庭院的风格，是中国保存最完好的晚清工商业古建筑群之一。目前，胡庆余堂开设了一个名医馆和一个中药博物馆，是传承和传播中医文化精粹的重要场所。

课堂思考与讨论

1. 胡庆余堂是一家什么企业？它的历史有多久？

2. 胡庆余堂为什么能成为"老字号"？

3. 你或你身边的人吃过中药吗？你们对中医药文化有什么看法？

4. 课后调查：中国人或外国学生是否听说过胡庆余堂，对中医药有什么看法?

5. 查资料,了解杭州或中国其他地区还有哪些著名的中药品牌。

6. 在你的国家是否有传统医药文化,发展情况怎么样?

Hu Qing Yu Tang

Hu Qing Yu Tang in Hangzhou is a traditional Chinese medicine enterprise with a long history, known as the "Medicine King of Jiangnan". It is one of China's existing time-honored traditional Chinese medicine enterprises, founded by Hu Xueyan, a businessman in the late Qing Dynasty, in 1874. In 1878, Xueji Traditional Chinese Medicine Store of Hu Qing Yu Tang was officially opened in Dajing Lane, Hangzhou, with 10 departments such as comprehensive department, pill-making rough material department, slicing department and original medicine storage. Later, the store moved to the riverside of the Qiantang River. After many years of operation, it was restructured into Hu Qing Yu Tang Pharmaceutical Co., Ltd. in 1999 and became a high-tech enterprise.

Hu Qing Yu Tang's initial prescription came from the presciptions of the Southern Song government-run medicine bureau, traditional prescriptions, prescriptions and secret recipes of famous doctors, etc. The main products include different dosage forms such as pills, powders, pastes, and pills. In the process of developing from traditional to modern, Hu Qing

Yu Tang exploits the advantages of traditional Chinese medicine, combines modern science and technology, draws lessons from the development experience of modern medicine and natural pharmacy, and constantly develops new products of traditional Chinese medicine, Chinese patent medicine and health food. Nowadays, Hu Qing Yu Tang has gradually developed from a traditional pharmaceutical enterprise into an industrial pattern integrating centralized cultivation of medicinal materials, processing of decoction pieces, production of medicinal wine, manufacturing of patent medicine, chain pharmacies, medical research, medicinal diet health care, TCM outpatient service, health tourism, etc. In 1996, Hu Qing Yu Tang was awarded the "China Time-honored Brand" certificate. In 2002, it was identified as China Famous Trademark. In 2006, Hu Qing Yu Tang Traditional Chinese Medicine Culture entered the first batch of National Intangible Cultural Heritage List.

The purpose of the establishment of Hu Qing Yu Tang is to benefit the society and to save the patients, meaning to benefit the people all of the world. Over the past hundred years, Hu Qing Yu Tang has been adhering to the pharmaceutical ancestral tenet of "genuine materials and fine pharmaceutical process", and the business philosophy of "sincere treatment and fair price", inheriting the integrity management spirit of "Jie Qi" (no cheat and establish a business with integrity), and its brand and cultural spirit are deeply rooted in the hearts of the public. The architecture of Hu Qing Yu Tang has the style of Jiangnan courtyard, which is one of the best preserved industrial and commercial ancient buildings of the late Qing Dynasty in China. At present, Hu Qing Yu Tang has set up a famous medical hospital and a traditional Chinese medicine museum, which is an important place to inherit and spread the essence of traditional Chinese medicine culture.

 Think and discuss

1. What kind of enterprise is Hu Qing Yu Tang? How long is its history?

2. Why can Hu Qing Yu Tang become a "time-honored" store?

3. Have you or anyone around you ever taken traditional Chinese medicine? What is your opinion on traditional Chinese medicine culture?

4. Do a survey and find out: Whether Chinese or foreign students have heard of Hu Qing Yu Tang, and what are their views on traditional Chinese medicine?

5. Check the information to find other famous traditional Chinese medicine brands in Hangzhou or other parts of China.

6. Is there a traditional medical culture in your country and how is its development?

课后练习

一、判断题

1. 胡庆余堂是一家中药企业。（　　　）

2. 胡庆余堂已经有近 150 年的历史了。（　　　）

3. 胡庆余堂一直只采用传统方式制作中药产品。（　　　）

4. 胡庆余堂只重视制作中药产品和开设中医门诊的业务。（　　　）

5. 胡庆余堂的产品剂型多样，包括丸、散、膏、丹等不同剂型。（　　　）

6. 民众非常信任胡庆余堂品牌。（　　　）

二、单选题

1. 胡庆余堂创办于中国_____。

A. 杭州　　　　　　B. 上海　　　　　　C. 北京

2. 胡庆余堂是在_____时期建立的。

A. 唐朝　　　　　　B. 明朝　　　　　　C. 清朝

3. "戒欺"的经营精神，它的意思是_____。

A. 对顾客诚信　　B. 救助病人　　　C. 注重保健

After-class exercises

I. True or false

1. Hu Qing Yu Tang is a Chinese medicine enterprise. (　　)

2. Hu Qing Yu Tang has a history of nearly 150 years. (　　)

3. Hu Qing Yu Tang has always made traditional Chinese medicine products only in traditional ways. (　　)

4. Hu Qing Yu Tang only pays attention to the business of making Chinese medicine products and opening Chinese medicine clinics. (　　)

5. The dosage forms of Hu Qing Yu Tang products are diverse,

including pills, powders, pastes, danes and other different dosage forms.
(   )

6. People trust Hu Qing Yu Tang brand very much. (   )

II. Single choice

1. Hu Qing Yu Tang was founded in _____, China.

A. Hangzhou   B. Shanghai   C. Beijing

2. Hu Qing Yu Tang was established during the period of the _____.

A. Tang Dynasty   B. Ming Dynasty   C. Qing Dynasty

3. The business spirit of "Jie Qi" means _____.

A. being honest toward customers

B. saving patients

C. focusing on health care